America the Unusual

America the Unusual

John W. Kingdon
University of Michigan

St. Martin's / WORTH

America the Unusual

Library of Congress Catalog Card Number: 98-84990
ISBN 0-312-18971-0 (paperback)
   0-312-21734-X (hardcover)
Printing: 1 2 3 4 5 02 01 00 99

Executive Editor: James R. Headley
Editorial Assistant: Brian Nobile
Production Editor: Douglas Bell
Production Manager: Barbara Anne Seixas
Project Coordination: Ruttle, Shaw & Wetherill, Inc.
Design Director: Jennie R. Nichols
Cover Design: Paul Lacey (Photo selection: Lucy Krikorian)
Cover Photo: U. S. Capitol Rotunda (detail).
   Copyright © J. McGuire/Washington Stock Photo, Inc.
Cover Printer: Phoenix Color Corporation
Composition: Ruttle, Shaw & Wetherill, Inc.
Printing and Binding: R. R. Donnelley & Sons, Inc.

Worth Publishers
33 Irving Place
New York, NY 10003

About the Author

J ohn W. Kingdon (B.A., Oberlin College; Ph.D., University of Wisconsin–Madison) has taught political science at the University of Michigan since 1965. In both teaching and research, he has concentrated on American government and politics and has specialized in legislative process and in public policy studies. He has also been a Guest Scholar at The Brookings Institution several times between 1969 and 1997.

Dr. Kingdon is a Fellow of the American Academy of Arts and Sciences and has been a Fellow at the Center for Advanced Study in the Behavioral Sciences and a John Simon Guggenheim Fellow. He has also been Chair of the Department of Political Science at the University of Michigan and President of the Midwest Political Science Association. He has served on editorial boards of several journals and has been an active participant in several professional associations.

Dr. Kingdon is the author of numerous books, articles, and papers and is a frequent lecturer around the United States and in other countries. His previous books include *Agendas, Alternatives, and Public Policies* and *Congressmen's Voting Decisions*.

To my students and colleagues

Contents

Preface

I have been teaching introductory American government courses at the university level for more than three decades. Students enter those courses with very little knowledge of or appreciation for governmental and political practices in other countries. Many of them seem to assume that (1) the United States is the norm, and (2) the United States is the best. In those assumptions, I believe that my introductory students resemble most American adults, to the extent that people think about these things at all.

As to what is "the best," reasonable people can differ, and my students and other Americans are entitled to their opinions. What is the norm, however, is not a matter of opinion. One major aim of my introductory course, and one of the aims of this book, is to point out that America is fundamentally different from other industrialized countries in many ways. Our constitutional system, the role of our political parties, the shape of our public policies, and the place of government in our economy and society are all most unusual, even peculiar.

I also invite readers to work on a puzzle with me: *Why* is America so different? As it happens, many scholars and other observers have wondered in print about the same thing, and there is quite a large body of writing about it. Various theories have been propounded and debated at length. I try in this book to arrive at some coherent answers to this question of why America is different, by surveying these rather diverse perspectives on American development, and by bringing them together into a framework of "path dependence." This synthesis concentrates on early events that sent America down its distinctive path, the subsequent conflicts over that path, and the choices that were made along the way, many of which reinforced the American differences.

Finally, I reflect in this book about the ways in which the American way of doing things serves us well or poorly. We are currently in the midst of a profound societal and political debate over the proper role of government. The two major political parties, for instance, are engaged in a fundamental struggle for the public policy soul of America. I hope that comparisons between America and other countries may shed some light on what works well and what doesn't. In some respects, as I will make clear, we are the envy of the world. In other respects, however, we are ill served by the way we approach governmental, social, and economic problems. The last chapter, therefore, argues for a tempering of American ideology and a return to pragmatism.

Those who have read my other books will recognize immediately that this one is different. Everything else I have written is in the nature of reports on my own original research. This book, by contrast, is in the nature of an extended essay. Instead of reporting the results of my own research, I attempt to synthesize others' works, although I do not claim to survey the massive literature comprehensively. I want to describe the differences between the United States and other countries, to reflect on why America is so different, to muse a bit about how our working assumptions affect our politics and policy, to explain how we came to make those assumptions, and to think out loud about the pluses and minuses of conducting ourselves as we do.

I have deliberately written this book to be accessible to a wide audience, ranging from students in introductory courses, to general nonacademic readers, to scholars. I have tried to write in an engaging style, and to construct a clear story from a rather complicated and even confusing body of writing on the subject, without being simplistic. I hope all types of readers, from those just generally interested in the subject to scholarly specialists, will find that they learn from this book, are stimulated to think more about why America is different, understand more fully the roots of those differences, and better appreciate the profound importance of our historical and current debates over the role of government.

A brief note on references. I have elected not to use footnotes in this book. Readers will instead find parenthetical references in the text that refer to works listed in the references section at the end of the book. So (Smith 1985) refers to a work cited there under the author Smith; (Smith 1985:132) refers to page 132 of that work.

I want to acknowledge the tremendous help of many individuals and institutions. I wrote this book during a couple of periods of leave at the Brookings Institution in Washington, D.C., which provided me not only with an office and a library but also, far more important, with a stimulating atmosphere and wonderfully productive interactions with many interesting and knowledgeable people. At the risk of slighting the contributions of many people at Brookings, I would like particularly to thank Margaret Weir, Kent Weaver, and Pietro Nivola for hours of conversations, suggestions for things I should read, willingness to bat around ideas, and arguments that refined my thinking. My colleagues and graduate students at the University of Michigan were also important sources of both general intellectual stimulation, as they have been throughout my career, and ideas about this particular project. Again at the risk of slighting a lot of people, I want to single out Terry McDonald as a particularly useful source of ideas and citations about the topics discussed in this book. Frank Baumgartner, Margaret Weir, Terry McDonald, Sharon Werning Rivera, Jim Kingdon, Kirsten Kingdon, and publishers' reviewers including James Anderson, Stephen C. Craig, and Rex C. Peebles, all provided wonderfully helpful and penetrating critiques of this manuscript, which improved the book substantially. I wish to thank my editors at St. Martin's/Worth, Beth Gillett and James Headley, for all of their help. None of these individuals and institutions are responsible for the interpretations and arguments contained in this book. I bear responsibility for any remaining errors in fact and judgment.

I owe so much to so many people. I have dedicated my previous books to my parents, who started me down my own path in life with great love and wisdom; to my wife and sons, who have surrounded me with love and support for a third of a century; and to my professors, who educated me with their extraordinary knowledge and intelligence. I dedicate this book to my students and colleagues, who have been sources of endless stimulation and fun through all these years.

John W. Kingdon

America the Unusual

1
___

Introduction

In 1994, my wife and I were visiting her most pleasant and friendly relatives in Norway. In the course of one of those lovely Norwegian encounters over coffee and sweets, I struck up a conversation with a niece, who was very pregnant at the time. I asked her what she was planning to do about her job when she gave birth. She replied that she would take a year's leave of absence, whereupon she would return to her job, which was guaranteed to be held for her. When I speculated that her husband's income would have to support the family during her leave, she replied that no, she would receive 80 percent of her salary during her year's leave. Surprised, as most Americans would be, I asked who pays for that. She replied in a rather offhanded manner, "the state," or what many Americans would call "the government."

I proceeded to tell her that in the United States, after years of struggle, we had just enacted a national family leave policy which provides a guaranteed, *unpaid* leave of absence for parents from their jobs for *twelve weeks* with guaranteed reinstatement. Now, this niece is an unfailingly polite young woman, and hardly politically involved or sophisticated. Still, she could barely disguise her wonder and even her amusement that the greatest and wealthiest country on earth could be so backward, at least from her point of view.

I later glanced out of the window at the busy Oslo street below. There on the corner was an Exxon station. Much like any other Exxon station in the world, this one posted its gasoline prices on a sign by the curb. A quick translation in my head from Norwegian kroner to dollars led me momentarily to believe that the price was about the same. But it didn't take even my addled brain long to realize that the price was stated in liters, not gallons. That is to say, gasoline in Norway cost roughly *four times* what it cost in the United States. I made some inquiries. It turned out that almost all of the difference in price was due to the extremely high taxes that the Norwegians levied on each liter of gas, at least high taxes by American standards. And this in a country awash in North Sea oil.

My eye-opening experiences at that charming family gathering in Oslo, Norway, as it happens, encapsulate the theme of this book. That theme can be directly stated: Government in the United States is much more limited and much smaller than government in virtually every other advanced industrialized country on earth. While there are some exceptions, in general the scope and reach of governmental programs in America is smaller. The taxes are lower, contrary to what many Americans might think. Public policies to provide for health care, transportation, housing, and welfare for all citizens are less ambitious. But other countries pay for their ambitious policies in the form of higher taxes, and in some cases more regressive taxes (Steinmo 1993).

Consistent with the comparatively limited reach of public policies, American governmental and political institutions are also limited. Our constitutional system of separation of powers and federalism is more fragmented and less prone to action, by design, than the constitutional systems of other countries. Our politics are more locally based, and centralizing features like cohesive national political parties are weaker than in other countries. This description of public policies, together with governmental and political institutions, adds up without undue distortion to one phrase: limited government.

Americans might well wonder why we are as we are. Do we have a distinctive political culture or dominant political ideology? Do we think differently from others, or value different things? If so, what are the differences? What has been the impact of early choices about governmental institutions, choices that still affect us today? Is there something about our social structure or economic arrangements that sets us apart? While not always definitively answered, these questions are all taken up in the pages of this book.

Even if America is different, should we want to be different? In the mid-1990s, as America approached the dawn of a new century, a struggle of titanic proportions was taking place over the proper role of government. Nowhere was that struggle more clearly fought than in the dispute between the Republican Congress elected in 1994 and President Clinton over balancing the budget—a dispute that shut down parts of the government in late 1995 and early 1996 for unprecedented lengths of time. Most Americans saw that gridlock over the budget as petty or "political," whatever they might have meant by that word. But there was nothing petty about it. At stake was nothing less than a fundamental clash of philosophies over what government's purposes should be, and what should be the reach and size of federal programs that profoundly affect almost every American.

One thing missing from that clash, it seems to me, was the recognition that American politics has a very different center of gravity from the politics of nearly every other industrialized country. Profound as our differences might be, the center of our politics still looks much less to government for solutions to whatever problems might occupy us, compared with the centers of other countries' politics. After all, the battle over the "Republican Revolution" of 1995–96 placed the American left well to the right of what most other countries would regard as their political center. As a general rule, Americans think that government should be much more limited than citizens of other countries do. And our governmental institutions were deliberately designed to accomplish that limitation.

We might do well to pause in the midst of our disputes to take stock of where we stand. Are taxes actually too high? To be a bit Goldilockian, is government actually too big, too small, or just about right? Or, to be more nuanced about it, in what *respects* is government too big, too small, or just about right? Looking to the experience of other countries won't provide the answers, because we would still have to decide for ourselves whether we want to continue on our unusual path, accelerate its limitations on government, or go in a different direction. But in the course of comparing ourselves to others, we might pick up some hints.

This book starts by simply describing the major differences between the United States and other advanced industrialized countries. In Chapter 2, we examine the facts: the institutions of government limited by the separation of powers, the weakness of our political parties in comparison with other countries, the smaller reach of our public policies, our lower tax burdens, and the general limited role of government in our collective social and economic life. We will also discuss some supposed exceptions to the general rule of limited government, such as the great commitment to public schooling, the burdens of regulation, the litigiousness of American society, and the size of our military establishment.

But these descriptions are not just isolated little facts. Some degree of agreement on a philosophy of limited government binds them together. So Chapter 3 attributes the factual differences between America and other countries to a prevailing American ideology. The tenets of this ideology are not shared by all Americans, and the center of this ideology is criticized from both the left and the right. We will notice that it's difficult even to think about who believes in these tenets. But I will argue that this prevailing American ideology can be described, has been quite stable through our history despite fluctuations from time to time, affects our institutions and public policies dramatically, and is above all distinctive. That is, despite our differences, Americans at the center of our politics do think differently from people at the center of other countries about the proper role, possibilities, and limits of government. An examination of this pattern of thinking will also try to make sense of the supposed exceptions to the general description of limited government. In Chapter 3, I will also try to sort through something that has occupied many scholars: the importance of institutions, as opposed to the importance of ideas, on the shape of public policy in the United States.

If Americans think differently, where did that thinking come from? Isn't it an interesting puzzle: *Why* is America so different? Chapter 4 attempts to trace our roots. We start with migration—why Americans came to this country in the first place, what concepts they brought with them, and how those concepts differed from those held by people who stayed behind. We discuss the remarkable diversity and localism in the United States. We include theories about economic and social structure— the absence of a feudal system, the distinctiveness of organized labor, and the workings of the American capitalist system. We consider features of American economic and noneconomic opportunity, the importance of social mobility, and the impact of the frontier. And we note the importance of isolation from other countries, which was created and maintained by the vast oceans separating us from other continents, but which has been fundamentally eroded by modern communications and transportation technology.

Here is a brief sketch of the theory I develop at the end of Chapter 4 to explain the differences between the United States and other industrialized countries. It's a version of a "path dependence" story (see Arthur 1988, 1994; North 1990), in which early events started us down the path along which we have been traveling ever since, and subsequent events reinforced our direction. We started with migration: Many of the early settlers in this country were systematically different from those who stayed behind in the old country. They brought certain distinctive ideas with them, especially their suspicion of hierarchy and authority, and hence their distrust of government. They also left behind the values of societies in which feudalism and aristocracy had produced legacies of class and privilege, holding instead to values of individualism and equality of opportunity. The founders of the country built these ideas into our governmental institutions, providing intentionally for a markedly limited government. We also started with the fundamental localism and diversity of America, which also prompted the founders to construct a limited government, particularly a limited federal government. So we started down our path because the values of the early immigrants, combined with localism and diversity, produced this powerful interaction between ideas and institutions.

Once that started, subsequent events reinforced our direction. These factors included some features of the American capitalist economic system, the distinctively nonsocialist cast of our labor unions and political parties, the opportunities provided by the frontier and other features that promoted social mobility, and our isolation from other countries.

This picture of path dependence does not mean that our directions were predetermined or inevitable. At various points in American history, there were profound struggles over the design of our governmental institutions and the shape of our public policies. We could have gone in different directions at those junctures—and indeed, we sometimes did. The New Deal of the 1930s, for instance, involved a great many "big government" changes. I discuss such critical points in our history in the course of developing the path dependence account.

Finally, we will reflect in the last chapter on what it all means. As we approach the new millennium, where do we stand? Can we learn something valuable from other countries? Does American ideology blind us to some productive possibilities, and if so, what are they? Could we benefit from less ideology and more pragmatism? To the extent that we understand why we have come to our current situation, do we want to alter what we do and how we do it? Is it possible to change direction, toward either more or less government, and if so, how? But should we want to change, or should we continue doing largely what we have been doing? Or will we be forced to change, whether we want to or not, by the inexorable march of demographics and global change? If so, how? Among other things, I argue in that last chapter that American ideology serves us well in some respects but ill in others, and that we could benefit from more pragmatism in our politics and public policy making.

So in the pages of this book, let's discover some facts about the United States compared with other countries, reflect on why America is so very unusual, and think together about what we can learn about our situation and what, if anything, we want to do about it.

2

Describing the Comparisons

Before we leap into interpretations and explanations, let's concentrate on the facts. In later chapters, we will try to understand why the United States is as it is, and how we might evaluate our practices. This chapter, however, simply describes the United States compared to other industrialized countries. We start with American governmental institutions, proceed to consider the strength of our political parties, and end with some observations on the patterns of public policy and the size of the public sector.

INSTITUTIONS

SEPARATION OF POWERS

American institutions are rooted in a system of separation of powers, in which government is divided into the familiar legislative, executive, and judicial branches. The Constitution, together with practices that have developed since the Constitution was adopted, provides for the independence of the branches in several ways. Members of the different branches are selected differently, for one thing: the president in four-year terms by nationwide popular vote and an electoral college, the House of Representatives in two-year terms by election from districts of roughly equal population, the Senate in six-year terms by popular election statewide, and the judiciary appointed for life by the president with Senate approval. The Constitution also assigns different powers of government to the different branches. But a system of checks and balances provides that each branch checks the others. So, for example, the president can veto acts of Congress, the courts interpret and can overturn acts of Congress, and Congress can check the executive branch by using its power of the purse.

While this description of our institutions is completely familiar to any high school student who has studied government in social studies or civics courses, many Americans don't appreciate how utterly peculiar our governmental institutions are. Virtually all other representative democracies in advanced industrialized countries use some version of a parliamentary system. In a traditional parliamentary system, there is no separation of powers. The head of state, usually called a prime minister or premier, is by definition the leader of the majority in the parliament. If one party controls the parliamentary majority, the leader of that party becomes the prime minister. If no one party controls the majority, the prime minister is named through a process of negotiation among the parties making up a majority coalition of parties.

In any event, the head of state is not separately elected nationwide. He or she runs in an individual parliamentary district, is the leader of the parliament, and particularly the leader of the parliamentary majority. There's also no fixed four-year term for the prime minister. The parliament can choose to oust the prime minister and cabinet, or the prime minister can dissolve parliament and call new elections. In either case, the process of forming a government begins anew. I was fond of pointing out to my students in 1995 that if the United States had a parliamentary system, there would be no president, the Senate would have no power to speak of, and the head of state would be Newt Gingrich.

This is, of course, a somewhat simplified picture. I don't mean to imply that the prime minister "follows" parliament, for instance. Indeed, the party discipline in such systems results in backbenchers (ordinary members of parliament) following their party's leadership—to a person, on most issues. I also presented a simplified comparison of the United States to other countries. Some countries, like contemporary France, have a hybrid system somewhere between a separation of powers and a parliamentary system. The president is elected nationwide and is granted substantial powers under the Fifth Republic constitution. But a second figure, the prime minister, is the leader of the parliamentarians in the majority coalition, and parliament has its own considerable powers. Israel recently adopted a hybrid system in which the head of state is elected separately from the parliamentary elections. In other countries, a nationally elected president is mostly a ceremonial figure except that he or she invites a given parliamentary leader to form the governing coalition. Some countries have a judiciary with virtually no independent governmental power; others have a judiciary with more substantial powers.

Still, the United States is very different. The president is elected separately from the Congress, serves for a fixed term unless impeached, and has a good deal of power independent of the Congress. Because the various bodies are chosen in different electorates and by different means, it's possible for one party to control the presidency and another to control one or both houses of Congress, a situation that is rendered impossible by definition in a strictly parliamentary system. Checks and balances really do operate in the American system. The Republicans in control of both houses of Congress in 1995 and 1996, for instance, found themselves checkmated by presidential vetoes. And President Clinton's proposals on many subjects in

1993 and 1994, even with fellow Democrats controlling both houses of Congress, often encountered vigorous congressional opposition, substantial modification, or even defeat. The deadlock of 1995–96 that resulted in the partial shutdown of the federal government would be constitutionally impossible in a conventional parliamentary system.

The bottom line is that the American constitutional structure is much more fragmented, and therefore less capable of taking coordinated action, than that of most other countries. Leaving aside the question of who is following whom—parliament or prime minister in the parliamentary case, president or Congress in the American case—the point is that there is a much greater degree of coordination between branches in a parliamentary system than in the American separation of powers system. Lipset (1990:21), after going through all of these consitutional provisions like separation of powers and checks and balances, summarizes the point thus: "No other elected national government except the Swiss is as limited in its powers."

FEDERALISM

As if the separation of powers weren't fragmentation enough, the American governmental system is further fragmented by federalism. Not only are powers of government divided at the national level among the three branches, but powers are also divided between the national government on the one hand and state and local governments on the other. In contrast to the unitary system found in some other countries, in which the regional governments are simply administrative units of the central government, the American federal system provides for states to have their own sovereign powers. The national government in the United States is a government of "enumerated" or "delegated" powers, meaning that constitutionally, the national government cannot do anything without a grant of authority for that activity in the Constitution. Powers other than those listed as powers of the national government are "reserved to the states or to the people" by the Constitution as amended. Exactly what those enumerated powers mean, of course, has been the subject of two centuries of constitutional interpretation, which has seen a considerable expansion of the federal role. Nevertheless, American-style federalism does limit the federal government to a list of powers and reserves other powers to state and local governments.

One manifestation of the federal system is the place of the United States Senate. During the constitutional convention, a monumental dispute arose between those who saw the new arrangement as that of a central government composed of equal states and those who viewed it as a more unitary central government with representation on the basis of population. The grand compromise was to create a bicameral Congress, in which one body (the Senate) had two senators per state regardless of population, and the other (the House of Representatives) was apportioned on the basis of population. In contrast to many countries, in which the upper house is largely powerless, the compromise provided that the two houses would be coequal in most major respects, and that legislation would have to be approved by both. Thus was federalism enshrined in the national institutions, as well as being provided in a division of power between national and regional governments.

Set in comparative context, federalism is not uniquely American. Whereas some countries have unitary systems, in which regional governments are actually administrative subdivisions of the central government, other countries have a federal system. Canada, for instance, operates with a combination of federal and parliamentary government.

But what is so distinctive about the United States is the combination of separation of powers with federalism. That combination makes for an extraordinary fragmentation, a remarkable inability to coordinate, and substantial blockages in the way of mobilizing government for action. There are legitimate differences of opinion about whether this extraordinary fragmentation is a good thing or not, as we will note when considering the pluses and minuses of the American way of doing business, but factually, that is the state of affairs.

IT'S NO ACCIDENT

America didn't just stumble into this constitutional fragmentation. As will be evident by the end of Chapter 3, the founders did not trust government authority. So they deliberately designed government to be weak. In part, their designed weakness took the form of explicit prohibitions on government activity, as in the Bill of Rights. In part, it took the form of deliberate fragmentation, so that no one part or level of government would have all the power and each of the parts would check the others.

The Constitution, of course, replaced the Articles of Confederation. It had come to be generally understood at the time that the Articles had fragmented power too much. States under the Articles, for instance, levied tariffs on each other, which necessitated the more central control over interstate commerce that was lodged in the powers of Congress by the Constitution. In several respects, the Constitution strengthened the hand of the central government.

Still, in comparison with most other industrialized countries, the American structure of governmental institutions is far more fragmented. This fragmentation makes it much more difficult to coordinate government action, to mobilize the various parts in a single direction, and to change the direction of public policy. Those consequences were not accidental. They were deliberately designed into the constitutional system. For some, that's the genius of the founders; for others, it's the curse of their legacy.

POLITICAL PARTIES

PARTIES IN LEGISLATURES

Given the all-out, bitter war between the parties during 1995 and 1996, with the impressive levels of party cohesion, readers may find the truth hard to believe. But compared to other countries, political parties in the United States are quite weak. In a parliamentary system, party members are expected to vote *to a person* with their party's leadership when the leadership insists on it. Even abstaining from such a vote, let alone voting with the opposition, is regarded as a dereliction of duty and is severely punished. Members of parliament have even been known to lose their seats, thus ending their political careers, because they abstained on issues deemed central to their party's leadership (e.g., Epstein 1964).

Compare that picture to the American case. Members of Congress are quite autonomous. They consider themselves responsible not to their party's leadership but to their own constituents. Party cohesion reaches sometimes impressive levels in the Congress, not because the leadership has much ability to sanction wayward members, but because common principles, similar constituencies, and electoral experiences bind members together (Kingdon 1989:120–123). Complete party cohesion is limited to certain procedural votes.

Consider David Bonior of Michigan, the second-ranking leader of the Democratic Party in the House of Representatives during the Clinton administration. He opposed his own party's president on the approval of the North American Free Trade Agreement, not only announcing his opposition and voting against it, but also actively working against approval. Bonior's behavior would be unheard of in a parliamentary system with strong parties. He would surely resign his party leadership position. If he didn't resign, he would be removed. Even if he were not in a leadership position, he probably would lose any standing he might have had in parliament and possibly would lose his seat. But in the United States, because we prize autonomy and responsiveness to members' own constituents, Bonior was not only tolerated but also encouraged by his Democratic Party colleagues in Congress and by just about everybody else. He was simply taking care of his labor union constituents working in the Michigan automobile plants, the thinking went, and American legislators are expected to do that.

Americans find the lockstep party discipline in other countries' parliaments quite odd. Why should legislators behave like sheep, we think, blindly following their party leadership? What are members of parliament, we ask? Cannon fodder? Warm bodies?

The answer is that this pattern of party discipline is, at its root, an alternative system of representation. Americans like to think of representation as a relationship between an autonomous legislator and his or her constituents. The legislator represents the interests of her or his own constituents, and if the constituents are not satisfied, they remove that individual legislator from office. If David Bonior is representing his own constituents, we argue, how dare the national party interfere? In a system of party discipline, by contrast, voters presumably vote for or against *parties* and the principles those parties stand for, not for or against individual politicians. Then the majority party or coalition should be cohesive enough to carry its program into effect. If those voters are not satisfied, the theory goes, they remove the *party* or coalition in power, and the governing party or parties are held accountable for their performance in government. Thus representation of popular preferences or interests is accomplished by the parties acting on behalf of a putative national majority, rather than by individual members of parliament acting on behalf of their own constituents. The parties, rather than individual politicians, are held accountable by the electorate.

In the United States, if members of Congress oppose their party leadership on a central issue, not much happens, as long as those members enjoy the support of their own constituents. But what if a member of parliament (MP) were to oppose his or her party leadership in a system of cohesive parties? First, that MP would run the risk of serious career damage within the parliament. The path to eventual cabinet status, for instance, might well be blocked. The only way for an ambitious politician to receive a cabinet appointment and ultimately to become prime minister in a parliamentary system, furthermore, is through faithful adherence to and leadership of the parliamentary party. Neither state or local office nor a prominent nonpolitical background can qualify an individual for advancement, as it can in the United States. Members of the U.S. House of Representatives who oppose the party leadership might run such a career risk as well, reducing their chance at a committee chairmanship, for instance, but the sanctions are neither as clear nor as inevitable. In the U.S. Senate, adherence to the seniority system renders even that possible sanction extremely unlikely. American party leaders simply do not have the same ability to affect their members' careers as parliamentary party leaders have.

Second, the wayward member of parliament in a strong party system might be called back to the local constituency party association, and even denied the party's renomination for parliament, a career-ending event. For instance, the importance of the local constituency party, not the national party, in enforcing party discipline in the British parliament (Ranney 1965; Epstein 1964) indicates how widespread is the expectation that parliamentarians will stand with their party. Throughout the country, locality by locality, everybody agrees that representation is supposed to be accomplished through parties rather than by individual members of parliament. That agreement is fundamentally different from Americans' expectations, which center much more on approval or disapproval of individual members of Congress. If our own representative's bonds with us are strong, our thinking goes, the party has no business interfering.

PARTIES AS ORGANIZATIONS

Not only are American political parties weaker in Congress than are parliamentary parties in other countries, but the parties are also weaker as organizations. Political parties the world over are fundamentally organizations that seek to win elections. But in the United States, individual candidates tend to their own campaigns. They make their own decisions about whether to run or not. They raise and spend their own campaign money. They make their own decisions about what positions they will take on the issues of the day. They work much more with paid consultants hired by their own campaigns than with party officials. They communicate with the electorate more through the media and through their own appearances, and less through party activists, than candidates in countries with stronger parties. They present themselves to the electorate as individuals, and the electorate judges their candidacies.

Let's not go too far. Parties are not meaningless in the United States. Voters often decide on the basis of their party loyalties or, if their loyalties are weak, at least consider party labels as they evaluate candidates. Parties do raise and spend substantial campaign funds, a fact that the orgy of contributions to the political parties in 1996 underlined. Parties also provide many campaign services to their candidates and play central roles in recruiting candidates and in nominations. Even though party cohesion in Congress rests more on agreement among like-minded partisans than on sanctions available to punish wayward members, cohesion can still be very impressive. In 1993, for instance, not a single Republican voted for President Clinton's budget in either House or Senate.

But we need to remember what we're addressing in these pages: We're trying to compare the United States to other industrialized countries—representative democracies in Europe, Canada, Japan, Australia, and so forth. Relative to those other countries, it's fair to say that parties are weaker organizations in the United States, in all of the ways I have suggested.

IT'S NO ACCIDENT

As with the case of the structure of governmental institutions, Americans didn't just stumble into relatively weak political parties. The founders wanted to avoid the evils of parties, even though parties emerged quickly after the founding. The discussion of faction in *The Federalist, No. 10,* for instance, is aimed in part at political parties. In the first part of the nineteenth century, furthermore, even though political leaders grudgingly tolerated parties, their aim was to crush the opposition and thus eliminate the need for party competition (Hofstadter 1969).

In retrospect, the emergence of political parties, and even their legitimation, was inevitable. No system of representative democracy that chooses leaders by elections and guarantees freedom of speech and association escapes political parties. Parties are not only inevitable, but also desirable, accompaniments to democratic institutions. Democracies need parties to organize elections and to govern institutions. So parties emerged and grew in strength over most of the nineteenth century.

Starting early in the twentieth century, however, and lasting to the present day, Americans deliberately set about to erode the power of political parties. The major agent of these changes in the first two decades of the twentieth century was the Progressive movement. Progressives saw as their mission a sharp attack on the wealthy and politically powerful, and thus an attack on big corporations, big finance, and big political machines. They saw parties as corrupt handmaidens of wealth and privilege, and an attack on parties was therefore a central part of their attack on economic and political power.

Progressive political reforms were aimed squarely at the political parties of the time. In the Congress, Speaker Cannon was overthrown in 1910, and the House of Representatives adopted such practices as the seniority system. These measures were designed to take powers, such as naming committee chairs, from the party leaders and to insulate wayward House members from retaliation by party leaders. The Constitution was amended to provide for direct election of senators and for woman suffrage. Both of those amendments broadened popular participation in elections, again eroding the power of party leaders.

From the point of view of weakening the political parties, the most significant reform of the Progressive era was the introduction and subsequent spread of direct primary elections. Instead of nominating candidates for all levels of office by party conventions or party caucuses, as had been the practice up to that time and still is the practice in many countries, state after state adopted direct primary elections. While primaries broadened popular participation in nominations, they also took nominations out of the hands of party leaders. Even presidential nominating conventions, formerly dominated by party activists, gradually became meaningless in the last half of the twentieth century, as more and more delegates were chosen by direct primary elections rather than by local and state party conventions. The erosion of the power of political parties by the spread of direct primary elections was not instantaneous, but instead took place gradually throughout this century, state by state and locality by locality. But the adoption of direct primaries, a major part of the Progessive agenda, did eventually result in the severe weakening of the parties.

Many urban party machines, and some rural machines as well, had also depended on a system of patronage, in which citizens couldn't get employment in the city government without the support of their neighborhood party official. Creation of career civil service systems across the country—federal, state, and local—knocked the props from under that system of party patronage. Again, reformers knew what they were doing: A career civil service based on such principles as "expertise" and "merit" was aimed squarely at the political parties (Shefter 1994:16). Many states and localities also provided for nonpartisan local elections and adopted provisions for citizens to initiate public policy changes at the ballot box. Again, these features weakened parties.

Each of these reforms had its own rationale, and each was designed to achieve laudable goals. It might also be argued that the weakening of political parties was an unintended side consequence of these reforms, and that the Progressives' major targets were concentrations of wealth and privilege and the broadening of popular participation. I personally think that the reforms were aimed squarely at the parties, and that they had their intended effects. But intended or not, gradually over the course of this century, party loyalties in the electorate declined, and campaigns became more candidate- and less party-centered. Despite the recent assertiveness of party leadership in Congress (Rohde 1991), the strength of party leadership in Congress has eroded over the longer sweep of the twentieth century. We could debate at length the respects in which this electoral, organizational, and legislative decline of parties was a good thing or not, and scholars and other observers have engaged in such a debate for decades. But, factually, the picture is pretty clear.

PUBLIC POLICY

First, let's look at the big picture. In his 1996 State of the Union address, President Clinton declared that "the era of big government is over." But the fact is that American government has never been as big as in other industrialized countries. That's true not just of the federal government. Combining federal, state, and local activity, government is much less involved in most aspects of social and economic problems than it is in other industrialized countries. Contrary to many Americans' assumptions, the state is less intrusive, our government programs are smaller and less far-reaching, our public sector is smaller relative to the private sector, and yes, our taxes are lower.

Americans debate at length about whether government *ought* to be smaller than it is. But in this chapter, let's content ourselves with noticing that it *is* smaller than in other countries. We'll have our chance to consider the "ought" question later. Here we present some examples, go on to note some exceptions to this general picture of small government, and then compare the overall size of the U.S. public sector to that of other countries. We explain later in the book why public policy turns out as it does and reflect on how things ought to be.

SOME EXAMPLES

Consider medical care (see White 1995a). In every industrialized country in the world except for the United States, the entire population is covered by health insurance. Some countries have government-run national health insurance. Others require employers to provide insurance for their employees and fill in the gaps with government programs. Most finance long-term care, which in the United States is government-financed only through Medicaid for the poor. Not only do these other countries cover the entire population with health insurance, but they also do it at far less total cost (government plus private cost) than we spend for health care in the United States.

Take transportation (Weaver 1985; King 1973). While not universal, government-owned and -operated railroads are common in other industrialized countries. Many of their governments sponsor national airlines. Mass transit is more completely developed in more of their cities than it is in American cities. Freight moves in and out of central terminals, coordinated across rail, truck, and other modes by government. Now this sort of transportation structure, both infrastructure and operation, costs a lot. The Swiss rail system, for instance, is fabulously convenient for passengers but also fabulously expensive. But it represents the collective Swiss decision to spend part of their national treasure on that sort of government program. Americans have not made such a collective decision.

This picture of transportation extends to public utilities in general, including not only transportation industries like railroads but also communications (e.g., telephones, cable television) and power generation and distribution (Temin 1991:88). In many other countries, utilities are either owned and operated by government, or are government sponsored monopolies. Instead of imposing nationalization or direct government control, the United States keeps such activities in the private sector, but regulates them through both federal and state regulatory commissions. Over the last couple of decades, furthermore, the deregulation movement has resulted in even less government involvement in regulation of utilities.

Beyond utilities, the United States ranks at the bottom of Western industrialized countries in the percentage of capital formation invested in, and the percentage of the work force employed in, public enterprises of all kinds (Weaver 1985:71). The absence of state-owned enterprises (e.g., nationalized industries or railroads) in America compared to many other countries adds to the relatively large private sector in the United States.

Let's turn to welfare (Lipset 1996:71,289). Americans complain about the top-heavy welfare state. But it pales in comparison with welfare programs in other industrialized nations. Most countries provide family allowances, paid maternal leave and day care, longer annual vacations, and more generous old age pensions than the United States does. As my anecdotes at the beginning of Chapter 1 about Norwegian maternity leave and gasoline taxes underlined, however, they pay dearly for them.

It isn't as though the United States has no welfare state at all. Starting with soldiers and mothers (Skocpol 1992), we have provided some sorts of benefits to some people. We do have AFDC (or its post-welfare reform substitute), food stamps, disability benefits, social security pensions, Medicare for the elderly, and Medicaid for the poor. There have also been fluctuations in our public policies over time. The New Deal period of the 1930s, for instance, introduced some radical public employment programs and social security provisions to deal with the Great Depression that were unknown in many other countries. And Americans provide for some sorts of welfare-state benefits privately, such as health insurance and pensions, as union-negotiated fringe benefits rather than government programs.

Desite that, however, it's still true that compared to other countries, the American welfare system, at the federal, state, and local levels combined, remains less ambitious, provides fewer types of benefits, makes fewer people eligible for those benefits, and costs less per capita or as a proportion of gross domestic product (GDP). And as the enactment of welfare reform legislation in 1996 indicates, the United States is currently reinforcing that pattern. Further, employer-paid fringe benefits, including health insurance and pensions, have been shrinking as the unionized proportion of the labor force has fallen. As Weir, Orloff, and Skocpol (1988:xi) summarize it, "The United States never has had, and is not likely to develop, a comprehensive national welfare state along West European lines."

I'm not necessarily arguing here that the United States should adopt programs to provide for a more lavish welfare state. Again, we're sticking to the facts in this chapter. I'm just highlighting the fact that our welfare programs are much less comprehensive, and cover fewer people and fewer sorts of contingencies, than welfare programs in other countries. Many other countries really do have what one of my respondents in an earlier study called a "lust-to-dust" welfare state, the likes of which Americans would hardly contemplate.

Look at housing (Heidenheimer, Heclo, and Adams 1983:88). In many countries, government owns and manages a fair chunk of housing units or provides various forms of encouragement (e.g., favorable tax treatment and subsidies) to cooperatives, unions, and other nonprofits to build housing. While there is some public housing in the United States, it's not nearly as extensive, does not house as large a proportion of the population, and does not account for as large a proportion of the housing stock as in other countries. Whereas nearly all housing in the United States is constructed by private builders, it is not uncommon in European countries for a third or half of dwellings to be built by government or by nonprofits with the aid of government (Heidenheimer et al. 1983:102). Indeed, the first Clinton budget provided for even less public housing in the United States, proposing instead to provide vouchers to poor people for use in the private housing marketplace. While there are American government housing subsidies (e.g., the income tax deduction for home mortgage interest), there still is less government involvement in housing than in other countries.

EXCEPTIONS

So far, our examples have pointed in the same direction. Public policies, we have seen, are less ambitious, and the reach of government is less
broad-ranging in the United States than in most other industrialized countries. But there are some policy areas that seem to be exceptions to this picture of unrelieved limited government.

One of those exceptions is education (Heidenheimer et al. 1983:21;
King 1973). America has a long tradition of public elementary and secondary schools. Most of their financing and policy control rests at the local
and state levels, with fairly limited and recent federal involvement. Still,
this long and revered tradition of public schools in America stands in contrast to many other countries' reliance on private and religious schools.
There's also a long American tradition of public higher education: universities, colleges, and normal schools, financed from state, and sometimes
local, tax revenues. In England, for a contrasting example, public universities are a comparatively recent development.

Another exception to the pattern of limited government in the United
States seems to be government regulation (Nivola 1997). Other countries
do regulate some sectors of the economy (e.g., labor relations and retail
trade) much more heavily than we do. But in certain areas (e.g., banking,
securities, environmental, civil rights regulation) our regulatory regimes
seem to be quite thorough. A considerable deregulation movement in the
United States, dating to the early 1970s, has actually accomplished a substantial degree of deregulation in such areas as transportation, communications, and banking. Still, in some respects, the reach of government regulation remains quite extensive. In broad outline, the United States has
deregulated in economic spheres but has maintained a considerable apparatus of social regulation (e.g., environmental regulation, civil rights)
(Nivola 1997).

The question of regulation is accompanied by a much broader phenomenon, the much-discussed litigiousness of America. Americans sue
one another a lot more than do people in other countries, and therefore
spend a lot more in anticipating, avoiding, defending against, and prose-
cuting lawsuits. There were about three thousand lawyers for every million
Americans in 1990, about twice as many per capita as in 1970. The United
States has three times as many lawyers per thousand persons as Germany,
ten times as many as Sweden, and twenty times as many as Japan (Nivola
1997:75). Tort costs were 2.3 percent of American GDP in 1991, nearly
twice the rate of the next-ranking country. Comparable rates were 1.2 percent for Germany; 0.9 percent for France, Canada, and Australia; 0.7 percent for Japan; and 0.6 percent for the United Kingdom (Nivola 1997:27).

Litigation and government regulation add considerable costs to doing
business in the United States. Some of the litigation is strictly private. But
much of it springs directly from deliberate government policies, providing

for class-action suits and enforcement of civil rights, consumer protection, malpractice, and other statutes by creating the right to bring suit rather than by relying on other sorts of enforcement practices. In America, lawyers do things that bureaucrats do in other countries (Kagan and Axelrad 1997).

Actually, litigation is built into our Constitution. We provide for a Bill of Rights, enforceable in court. Our tradition of civil liberties, including the rights accorded criminal defendants, is much more rigorous than in many other countries. The equal protection and due process clauses of the Fourteenth Amendment have generated tremendous volumes of litigation. More broadly, the United States is built on a regime of individual rights, which requires a considerable legal apparatus to implement. As Tocqueville (1835) observed long ago, "There is hardly a political question in the United States which does not sooner or later turn into a judicial one."

Another exception can be found in the criminal justice system. Our rate of incarceration is by far the highest in the Western world. The various levels of government in the United States spend considerably more on police, courts, and prisons than other countries do, and those expenditures are growing. Some of the difference might be due to higher crime rates and stiffer penalties. But we also criminalize some activities (e.g., prostitution, gambling, marijuana use, environmental damage, some abortions) that other countries do not treat as criminal. We even tried prohibition of alcoholic beverages by constitutional amendment.

A final exception to the general maxim of limited government is, of course, the defense establishment. The United States maintains a much larger military than most other countries, with military expenditure consuming a substantial portion of the federal budget and GDP. Spending on national defense and veterans, for instance, accounted for about one-fifth of total federal government outlays in the fiscal year 1996. That proportion has been declining over the last several years, but it is still substantial.

All of these examples—education, regulation, litigation, criminal justice, and defense—seem to be exceptions to the rule of limited government in the United States compared to other countries. What accounts for these apparent anomalies? Actually, it turns out that most of them flow quite naturally and consistently from American conceptions of the proper role of government. Let's leave that observation dangling tantalizingly for now, and return to it in the next chapter.

THE SIZE OF THE PUBLIC SECTOR

Stepping back from the examples of public policy differences, what do they all add up to? How big is American government? The short answer is that American government is smaller, relative to the total size of the economy, than government in other countries.

American government has grown during the twentieth century. Although some of this expansion has been gradual, other growth has come along in big spurts. In the 1930s, the federal government added social security, agricultural assistance, several types of economic regulation, and other government programs to the total. In the 1960s it added Medicare, Medicaid, federal aid to education, and civil rights laws to the books. So we should notice first that government is bigger than it used to be.

But the total is still small by world standards. Let's look at some numbers. In 1995, the general government total outlays were 33 percent of GDP in the United States (federal, state, and local combined), 43 percent in Great Britain, 50 percent in Germany, 54 percent in France, 61 percent in Denmark, and 66 percent in Sweden (OECD 1996). To make this comparison less tied to these particular countries, the total of general government outlays throughout all the European Union countries amounted to 50 percent, compared to the 33 percent figure for the United States—a difference of 17 percentage points. Lest readers think that this picture is a peculiarity of 1995, the percentage point difference between the United States and Europe has been roughly similar every year since the late 1970s—ranging from a low of 13 percentage points in one year (1980) to a high of 17 in three years (1993, 1994, 1995), and averaging a 15 percentage point difference. In general, the difference between the United States and Europe has been widening, not narrowing (see also Rose 1991). There may be an ever so slight narrowing of the gap between the United States and European countries in the next couple of years, according to OECD projections, but the differences are still quite striking.

The differences in government outlays are doubly striking because the portion of the American budget allocated for defense is larger than in most other countries (Rose, 1991). In other words, if we were simply to compare nonmilitary outlays as a percentage of GDP, the American government would look even smaller in comparison to other industrialized countries.

These figures on government outlays do not include the effects of tax expenditures. It's possible that in the United States, we might provide government help for certain activities in the form of tax deductions or tax credits rather than direct government subsidies. Instead of government payments to the opera, for instance, we allow a charitable deduction for those who choose to contribute to the opera, but it's a government subsidy either way—whether as a direct payment or as tax revenue forgone. Instead of building a great deal of public housing, to take another example, we provide homeowners with a mortgage interest tax deduction.

Howard (1997) argues that including tax expenditures in the total would boost the size of the American welfare state. While it is probably true that taking account of tax expenditures closes some of the gap between the American and European public sectors, the general picture of a smaller American government is still largely accurate. Other countries also use tax expenditures to some degree, for one thing. And other coun-

tries start with such a markedly different approach to government authority and responsibilities that we would have to go a great distance through
tax expenditures to close the gap.

Furthermore, the fact that the United States tries to accomplish collective purposes through tax deductions and credits rather than direct government subsidies more than other countries do is an interesting commentary on the American way of doing business. We shy away from "big
government" in the form of subsidies, in other words, and try to hide such
expenditures by subsidizing various sorts of activities through manipulat-
ing the tax code. In the process, ironically, we make the tax code
grotesquely complex and government far less efficient.

Tax expenditures are also more regressive than direct government subsidies would be. "Regressive" means that wealthier people benefit more
than poorer people do, proportionate to their income. Take the tax deduction for mortgage interest, for example. Because wealthy people are in
higher tax brackets than poorer people, they get a larger percentage tax
expenditure subsidy for equal amounts of mortgage interest. They also
purchase more expensive houses and have larger mortgages, adding to the
subsidy they receive in the form of their mortgage interest deduction.

Much of the time, it would be more straightforward to subsidize than
to provide for tax deductions and credits. Instead of enacting the complicated provisions for tax deductions and credits for higher education that
President Clinton proposed, for instance, he could much more simply have
proposed straight subsidies and scholarships. As the example of mortgage
interest deduction shows, furthermore, subsidies are also sometimes fairer.
But the American impulse to avoid "big government" leads to some peculiar distortions.

If one compares total government tax receipts, rather than total government outlays, to GDP in these same countries, the picture is roughly
similar. To return to our comparison year of 1995, the tax receipts in the
United States (federal, state, and local) totaled 31 percent of GDP, compared to 45 percent for the total of European Union countries (OECD
1996). Some European countries were lower than the overall European
percentage (e.g., Great Britain at 38 percent), and others were considerably
higher (e.g., Sweden at 58 percent). Again, the estimates and projections
into 1996 through 1998 were almost exactly the same, the differences
between the American and European numbers have been maintained with
minor year-to-year variations since the late 1970s, and the gap between the
United States and the European countries has widened slightly over that
period.

THE BIG PUBLIC POLICY PICTURE

The public policy differences between the United States and other
industrialized countries can be summarized quite simply without doing

much violence to reality. Other countries provide more government services, pay higher taxes, and have larger public sectors relative to their private sectors. There seem to be a few exceptions to that general picture, but
mostly, those are the facts.

Not every scholar interprets the data in the same way as I have here.
Rose (1991), for example, argues that America is not alone in being what
he calls a "Rich Nation with a Not-So-Big Government." Other such countries are non-European nations along the Pacific Rim, such as Canada,
Japan, and Australia; the European ones are Switzerland and Finland. He
thus calls into question the notion that America is unique. Wilson (1998)
also questions the idea that America is the world's exception. Indeed, it has
become common in the literature on "American exceptionalism" to claim
that all countries are exceptional in some respects, and therefore to deny
the notion that America is different.

I think this is all a matter of comparison. Some countries, like the
Scandinavian ones, are extremely far from the United States on all of the
indicators, quantitative and nonquantitative, that we have been discussing.
Other countries are closer to the United States, and they make up Rose's
category of "Rich Nations with a Not-So-Big Government." But in some
respects, some of these countries are still very different from America,
despite being included in the same category. Canada has universal single-
payer health insurance, for instance; Japan has a much more centralized
economy and governmental decision-making process than America; and
Switzerland has a far more complete system of public transportation. The
United States also devotes much more of its public expenditure (as a percentage of GDP) to defense than other countries do, as Rose points out,
which means that on most major nonmilitary programs, the United States
is not nearly as ambitious as the overall figures might indicate.

I don't want to go so far as to argue that the United States is utterly
unique or exceptional. But I do think that America is very unusual among
industrialized countries in many respects, and that those respects are
important. I also find the question of *why* America is unusual both interesting and intriguing, because it tells us a lot about ourselves and about
how countries develop. I believe too that answers to that question can help
us to think about where we want to direct ourselves as a nation.

CONCLUSION

In this chapter, we have described several ways in which the United States is
different from other industrialized countries. Its governmental institutions
are more fragmented, its political parties are weaker, and the scope of its
public policy and size of its government are smaller. Why is this so? We
start to answer that question in the next chapter.

3

American Ideology

On another trip in Europe, my wife and I encountered some young students one evening. Over a convivial pitcher of beer (actually, several pitchers) we got to talking about different societies and cultures. One of these young men, perhaps emboldened by the quantity of beer he had consumed, leaned across the table and asked, "Tell me—what is America *really like?*"

I don't know about you, but I had no good answer on the spur of the moment. As is my unfortunate pattern, however, I thought of the right answer several hours later. If I had had my wits about me, I would have replied that there is no single America. I would have elaborated on the theme of diversity—how America is both New York City and rural Nebraska, how both mind-boggling affluence and grinding poverty exist in the same country, how America is beset by a bewildering array of racial, ethnic, regional, and other conflicts. Alas, I have never been asked that question since, but I do have a good answer ready now, in case anybody else should ask.

I realize that the United States is pluralistic, diverse, and fragmented in many respects. Nevertheless, I believe that Americans at the center of our politics think differently about the proper role of government than citizens at the centers of other industrialized countries do. In other words, it is fair to speak of a prevailing American ideology, which concentrates on limiting the power and reach of government. So the first cut at explaining why the United States is different from other industrialized countries is that we *think* differently. We have a different view of the proper authority, limits, and possibilities of government.

Alert readers will notice that I inserted the phrase, "at the center" of our politics, compared to the center of other countries' politics. Let's be clear what I mean by a "prevailing American ideology." I do not mean that all Americans hold to the same set of values. Indeed, as we will see, there have been quite different strains of American political thought through our history. I certainly do not want to argue that what I will characterize as a prevailing American ideology constitutes a dominant, hegemonic orien-

23

tation that drives out all other ideas. Far from it, indeed; there have been dramatic struggles over those ideas through the years.

The tenets of a prevailing American ideology, in my view, are widely shared at the center of our politics, and that center differs from the center in other countries. But I do not mean that every American agrees with these principles—far from it. Critics on the left, stretching from liberals to democratic socialists, believe that government should be much less limited. Critics on the right, from conservatives to libertarians, believe that government should be even more limited, at least in the realm of economics. (Some rightist critics, including the "religious right," favor more vigorous government regulation in social or moral spheres like abortion.) In the middle of the conventional left-to-right spectrum, however, I believe we can identify some shared ideological tenets. So by the term "prevailing" I mean that, despite our differences, the *center* of American politics distinctively favors limited government *more than* the political centers in other industrialized countries do.

There are also obviously a number of large, ambitious government programs in the United States. We do have a social security system, health insurance for the elderly and the poor, and the like, and those programs have been growing. But again, it's a matter of comparing our programs to those in other countries, which by and large are even more ambitious.

So when I speak of a "prevailing American ideology," I refer to the central tendency of our politics, not to the full dispersion of views around that center. I also concentrate on comparisons of American practices and ideas to those of other countries, rather than comparisons to some sort of ideal concept of what the size and reach of government should be. The intent of the chapter is to characterize the center of American politics and to argue that this center differs from the center of other countries.

I will elaborate on the content of that ideology in a moment, but let me first indicate its characteristics. First, "ideology" as I use the word does not necessarily mean a highly integrated, consistent belief system (Converse 1964). Depending on your tastes, you may prefer to think of a "body of ideas" or "philosophy" or "American thinking" or "political orientation." While I will use the word "ideology" as my shorthand, I hope that readers will not get hung up on the considerable scholarly controversies (see Kinder 1983) that swirl around the meaning of that word and the extent to which one finds ideological thinking in the mass public.

Second, the prevailing American ideology I will discuss has been quite stable over our history. Of course there have been changes. But a belief that government should be limited did not start with the congressional election of 1994. One finds a good deal of this thinking in the writings and speeches of the founders, for instance, and in the observations of Tocqueville in the early nineteenth century. We have fluctuated some, of course, swinging pendulum-style from bigger to smaller government and back again (Hirschman 1982, Schlesinger 1986). The patterns of our public policies have also shifted through time, particularly in the direction of larger government in the 1930s and 1960s. Nevertheless, I will try to trace some continuity through our history, particularly continuity as compared to other countries.

Third and most important, the prevailing American ideology is distinctive. It's quite different from the working assumptions of most other countries. Even if we were to concede that there's a lot of difference of opinion in America, and that there has been considerable fluctuation over time, the central tendency of American political culture could still be distinctive. I argue that it is, in fact, particularly in the sense that American politics has a different center of gravity from the politics of other industrialized countries, a center that stresses limited government.

Let us now characterize that center of gravity, examining the tenets of this prevailing American ideology. We start by describing the content of this ideology. We then see what results flow from this American way of thinking about the role of government. In the course of that consideration of results, we'll be able to find some coherence in the differences between the United States and other industrialized countries that we described in the last chapter and summarized roughly as a pattern of limited government. We'll also be able to figure out why the "exceptions" to that description emerge. In other words, we'll develop an explanation for the differences between America and other countries, an explanation rooted in this American ideology. Finally, this chapter will examine the effects of these ideas, as opposed to the effects of institutions, on the shape of American public policy. Actually, we will observe that the issue is not so much "ideas as opposed to institutions" as it is "ideas in combination with institutions." In the next chapter we will speculate about where American ideology came from.

THE CONTENT

There have been many attempts to distill the essence of American political thought into a list of themes. Huntington (1981:14), for instance, says that the content of what he calls "the American Creed" includes constitutionalism, individualism, liberalism, democracy, and egalitarianism. Lipset notes in one book (1979) that the most important of American values are equality and achievement; in another (1990:26) he observes, "The American creed can be subsumed in four words: antistatism, individualism, populism, and egalitarianism"; then in a third (1996:31), "The nation's ideology can be described in five words: liberty, egalitarianism, individualism, populism, and laissez-faire." McCloskey and Zaller (1984:1) start their study of "the American ethos" with the following observation: "Two major traditions of belief, capitalism and democracy, have dominated the life of the American nation from its inception."

I don't know quite what to make of such lists. For the purposes of our discussion in this book, however, I will start with two aspects of American political thought, individualism and equality, because these two categories tend to include a lot of the other ideas that scholars have identified as significant parts of American political thought. As readers will see, for instance, our discussion of individualism will take us into other streams of American thinking (e.g., communitarianism). We will eventually conclude that various streams actually converge on a distinctive distrust of authority and preference for limited government. Similarly, our consideration of equality will consider various aspects of equality (e.g., equality of result versus equality of opportunity). As it turns out, many of the values on others' lists are closely connected to the central themes of individualism and equality. We will notice, for instance, that liberty, laissez-faire, capitalism, and antistatism are related to individualism, and so we will discuss them within that category.

INDIVIDUALISM

Many observers have remarked that Americans emphasize individual goals and individual advancement, rather than community goals or the advancement of public or collective purposes. This individualism is closely connected to the much-noticed tendency of Americans to prize liberty or freedom, that is, liberty or freedom for autonomous individuals. We mean freedom from authoritarian restraint, the dictates of hierarchy, or governmental limits. As McCloskey and Zaller (1984:18) point out, "No value in the American ethos is more revered than freedom. The rights of individuals to speak, write, assemble, and worship freely, to engage in occupations and pastimes of their own choosing, and to be secure from arbitrary restraints on their conduct are central to the nation's democratic tradition."

Hofstadter (1989:xxxvii) continues this theme. He argues that despite the differences between agrarian and industrialist, working class and upper class, there is an underlying unity in American thought centered on "the natural elevation of self-interest and self-assertion." He goes on: "The major political traditions have shared a belief in the rights of property, the philosophy of economic individualism, and the value of competition; they have accepted the economic virtues of capitalist culture as necessary qualities of man." Hofstadter (1963:227) also describes a traditional American "distrust of authority," which at various points in American history has been turned against political machines, big business, and government itself. This distrust, he claims, "gave tenacity to the most ardent supporters of the Revolutionary War. It helped impede the adoption of the Federal Constitution, it was invoked to justify secession, it caused Americans to postpone into the twentieth century governmental responsibilities that were assumed decades earlier among other Western societies."

Hartz (1955), to take another example, argues that a "liberal" ideology built on individualism dominated American political thought right from the beginning. (The term "liberal" in this context obviously is not the current popular usage—it means a philosophy of limited government, built on high value placed on individuals and individual rights.) He says that his analysis is based on "the storybook truth about American history: that America was settled by men who fled from the feudal and clerical oppressions of the Old World." (Hartz 1955:3) He goes on to develop his notion that American political thought found its roots in the writings of John Locke, who stressed the primacy of the individual, the importance of individual rights, and an insistence on imposing limits on authority in general, and governmental authority in particular, to further those individual rights. Hartz (1955:39) says that Americans had "a frame of mind that cannot be found anywhere else in the eighteenth century, or in the wider history of modern revolutions."

In contrast to this emphasis on individualism and liberalism (classically defined), other historians and political philosophers maintain that the early Americans and the founders were motivated by more communitarian, republican values. In this context, the term "republican" refers neither to the modern Republican Party nor to a system of representative government that stands counter to direct democracy. It refers instead to a community in which people, including elected officials, deliberate together to pursue their conception of the public good. By this reckoning, American political thought was not predominantly individualistic. Indeed, Americans placed a high value on community and devotion to the public good, sometimes called "civic virtue."

Wood (1969:53), for instance, argues: "The sacrifice of individual interests to the greater good of the whole formed the essence of republicanism and comprehended for Americans the idealistic goal of their Revolution. From this goal flowed all of the Americans' exhortatory literature and all that made their ideology truly revolutionary." Wood (1969:58) goes on to clarify what a pursuit of the public good entailed: "This common interest was not, as we might today think of it, simply the sum or consensus of the particular interests that made up the community. It was rather an entity in itself, prior to and distinct from the various private interests of groups and individuals." Pocock (1975) traces this republican tradition not to Locke's theories but to Aristotle's assumption that man is social by nature, and to Machiavelli's notions of civic virtue versus corruption.

A variant of the republican reading of the Revolution and the founders' ideas holds that America started out republican in the eighteenth century, but that a liberal ideology of individualism and limited government subsequently supplanted the original ideas and came to dominate the nation's political thought. Young (1996:11), for instance, argues that Hartz overreaches by claiming that liberalism dominated American political thought right from the beginning; he maintains that it gradually gained dominance later. Wood (1992:326) dates the change to the early nineteenth century, culminating in the War of 1812, which heightened Americans' "pursuit of individual self-interest" (Wood 1992:327). In Wood's telling, the concept of the individual changed from individuals as civic beings to individuals as self-interested. Shain (1994:6) says, "America changed from being relatively communal in the 18th century to being far more individualistic in the 19th century." Sandel (1996:5) believes that liberalism—the notion that individual rights should be most important and that government should be limited—is "a recent arrival, a development of the last forty or fifty years." This version of liberalism, Sandel (1996:5) argues, gradually displaced its rival, a version of republican theory that had held sway earlier in American history, which required "a sense of belonging, a concern for the whole, a moral bond with the community whose fate is at stake." Common to these writers is the notion that despite the intellectual origins of the country, a more liberal, individualistic culture came to dominate American politics.

Other writers argue that neither liberalism nor republicanism aptly characterizes early American political thought. Shain (1994), for instance, maintains that a kind of religious communalism found in local, agrarian Protestant communities dominated eighteenth-century political thought. These local religious communities were not individualistic, Shain argues, in that they required the submergence of individual rights and wants in the community. Neither were they republican, he claims, in that they rejected such republican assumptions as attaining meaning through political and civic activity.

Still other recent authors argue that the dichotomy between liberalism and republicanism is artificial, and that the founders were actually quite skillful at combining them. Zuckert (1994:319) analyzes the writings of Locke and his contemporaries, from whom the founders freely borrowed, and argues that these writings are best characterized as designs for a "liberal republic." Zundel (1995:11) also holds that the "stark dichotomy" between liberal/individualistic and republican/communitarian traditions is "artificial and misleading," and that the two traditions borrowed freely from each other.

Other authors maintain that the various strains of American political thought, far from being compatible, actually coexist in a state of tension. Morone (1990:1), for instance, is struck by the importance of "The Democratic Wish," as he calls it, in which Americans both dread governmental power as a threat to their liberties and at the same time yearn for direct, communal democracy. He maintains (Morone 1990:18) that "liberalism is dominant," but that it is "repeatedly challenged by a recurring, subordinate ideology," a "communitarian spirit" (Morone 1990:73), which nevertheless is not really at the center of American politics. Bellah et al. (1985) also find a considerable tension between individualistic self-reliance and a yearning for community and meaningful relationships.

Smith (1993) points to what he calls "multiple traditions" in America, including such ugly ones as nativism, racism, and sexism. He argues that these do not lie "outside" American thinking, but are actually very much a part of it. Smith (1993:549) believes that "American political culture is better understood as the often conflictual and contradictory product of multiple political traditions than as the expression of hegemonic liberal or democratic political traditions."

Racism in particular continues to affect both American society and public policy. Quadagno (1994) argues that the 1960s War on Poverty, for instance, at first enjoyed a high degree of public approval. But as its beneficiaries became identified more and more as racial minorities, public support waned. According to this logic, welfare programs like AFDC also became more unpopular, as the stereotypical recipient according to public perception was an African-American unwed mother, even though in fact there were many more white than African-American welfare recipients. Opponents of welfare, job training, federal aid to urban areas, and other "big government" programs in both the 1930s and 1960s skillfully used American racism, the argument runs (Quadagno 1994:191,196), to buttress their more general antigovernment position by suggesting that the programs disproportionately benefited African-Americans. Opposition to the welfare state, therefore, has not simply been a straightforward expression of antigovernment ideas, this notion would have it, but has also been reinforced by a tradition of racism in America.

For the purposes of this book, I find it impossible, and probably unnecessary, to wade into, let alone settle, these disputes about the various traditions in American political thought and about the founders' philosophies. Whether the founders and subsequent Americans were liberal individualists or republican communitarians, or even driven by racism, I would argue that in the main they were still suspicious of government, skeptical about the benefits of government authority, and impressed with the virtue of limiting government.

On the face of it, individualists would think that way. They would emphasize private, individual advancement and individual rights and freedoms, and they would see considerable potential for government tyranny, which must be controlled. But even some of the more communitarian types, concentrating as they did on the local autonomy of religious communities, might think in quite similar ways about government threats to their freedom to live as they would like and as they believe is moral and right. And beyond the religious communities, it might be quite possible for deliberative republicans, interested in the common good, to reason together and come to the conclusion that government should be limited. As we will see in a moment, in fact, the writings of the founders do look a lot like that.

Both liberal and republican traditions, in other words, argue for limited government, each in its own way (Morone 1990:29). After reviewing the sometimes incompatible strains in American political thought, Huntington (1981:33) summarizes the point:

> Logically inconsistent as they seem to philosophers, these ideas do have a single common thrust and import for the relations between society and government: all the varying elements in the American Creed unite in imposing limits on power and on the institutions of government. . . . The distinctive aspect of the American Creed is its antigovernment character. Opposition to power, and suspicion of government as the most dangerous embodiment of power, are the central themes of American political thought.

Again, we need to remind ourselves that we're thinking of America in comparative perspective. Of course we have by now built a version of the welfare state, of course the federal government's authority and reach has grown over the course of our history, and of course not all of these intellectual strains can be neatly subsumed into some sort of hegemonic ideology. But in this book, we're trying to understand America *relative to* other industrialized countries, not relative to some absolute sense of what would constitute a limited government. So I'm not trying to characterize American government as limited in some absolute sense or to claim that classical liberalism is the only hegemonic American political ideology. I'm simply arguing that the center of American political thought is considerably to the right of the center in other countries (using the label "right" in its contemporary colloquial sense of having a preference for smaller, more limited government).

Let's look at the founders for a moment. An excellent window into their political thought is *The Federalist*, a collection of essays originally published in the New York press in 1787–88. These essays were written to support the adoption of the Constitution of the United States, under which Americans still live today. The essays were published anonymously under the name Publius, but it soon became apparent that the authors were Alexander Hamilton, James Madison, and John Jay. In addition to offering popular polemics in favor of the Constitution, these essays were quite remarkable statements of the founders' political philosophy, the intellectual underpinnings of the form of government which they designed.

They start with some pessimistic assumptions about human nature. "If men were angels," says *The Federalist, No. 51*, "no government would be necessary." But in the next sentence, they realize that government must not only control people's excesses but must itself also be controlled: "If angels were to govern men, neither external nor internal controls on government would be necessary." So both kinds of control are necessary: "You must first enable the government to control the governed; and in the next place oblige it to control itself."

The main device for accomplishing this control of government is to provide that no one part of government have a disproportionate share of power. Thus government powers are separated into different branches, each checking the other, and into national versus regional governments. As *The Federalist, No. 51,* sums it up, "Ambition must be made to counteract ambition."

One purpose the founders wanted their new governmental structure to accomplish was to "cure the mischiefs of faction" (*The Federalist, No. 10*), the tendency to faction being a "dangerous vice" in their view. Madison defined a faction as "a number of citizens, whether amounting to a majority or minority of the whole, who are united and actuated by some common impulse of passion, or of interest, adverse to the rights of other citizens, or to the permanent and aggregate interests of the community." The authors of *The Federalist* believed that the causes of faction were "sown in the nature of man," and particularly in "the various and unequal distribution of property." That belief brought them inescapably to the conclusion that "the *causes* of faction cannot be removed, [so] relief is only to be sought in the means of controlling its *effects.*"

They used two major means: republican government and separation of powers. By "republican," in this usage of the word, they meant representative democracy as opposed to direct democracy. *The Federalist, No. 10,* discusses the dangers of direct democracy at length, and argues that it really can only work in small, contained settings like ancient Athens or New England town meetings. For larger polities like the new union, the people must elect representatives to act on their behalf. Their constitutional design provided for such direct election to the House of Representatives, and for indirect selection of senators (by state legislatures) and the president (by an electoral college). A major point of *The Federalist, No. 10,* was that in the founders' view, the excesses of majority faction could be controlled by these mechanisms of representation and by the insulation of government from direct democracy. And minority factions would be balanced by the majority rule inherent in elections.

The other means of controlling the effects of faction was the separation of the powers of government into different branches—legislative, executive, and judicial—and the provision of a federal system—the division of powers between national and state/local levels. At the same time, the founders provided for the famous principle of checks and balances, in which the different branches and levels would limit one another. That way, no faction, majority or minority, could capture control of the entire apparatus. Thus *The Federalist, No. 39,* points out that the republican form of government the founders envisioned "derives all its powers directly or indirectly from the great body of the people," thus limiting minority faction. But the division of its powers by the separation of powers, by a bicameral Congress, and by federalism combats popular power and majority faction. Indeed, *The Federalist, No. 47,* claims that "the accumulation of all powers, legislative, executive, and juidiciary, in the same hands, whether of one, a few, or many, and whether hereditary, self-appointed, or elective, may justly be pronounced the very definition of tyranny."

Running through all of these ideas about the proper design of government are two themes. One is a desire to found government on the direct or indirect sovereignty of the people. The Federalists who drafted the 1787 Constitution created a political theory positing a direct link between the people and the national government that bypassed the states. But that government was representative rather than direct democracy (Wood 1969). The idea of sovereignty of the people, however, was combined with the second theme: profound suspicion of popular control of government. In the founders' design, for instance, the House of Representatives was the only part of the new national government that was directly elected.

Beyond those two themes, the institutions are grounded in an insistence that tyranny, whether from a majority or a minority, be combated, and that individual rights and privileges be protected from a potentially tyrannical government. Regardless of the balance or ascendancy between individual and communitarian values in American political thought, the result is a suspicion of authority and an emphasis on limited government.

EQUALITY

Sometimes it takes an outsider to understand. Alexis de Tocqueville was just such an outsider. A French aristocrat, he traveled in the United States for nine months in 1831–32. His observations during these travels were the basis for his much-acclaimed *Democracy in America*. Far from a simple description of America in the 1830s, this book is a remarkably shrewd commentary on American politics and society that still deserves our attention today.

Tocqueville was very much struck by the individualism that we have been discussing. Indeed, McCloskey and Zaller (1984:111) say he coined the word: "When Tocqueville set out to characterize the novel social orientation he found in the United States in the 1830s, he described it as 'individualism.' Although the word seems never before to have appeared in the English language, it so aptly characterized American culture that within a few years it was widely accepted as one of the nation's most distinctive traits."

Tocqueville also noticed a rich and diverse American civil society. By "civil society" most people mean a kind of "third sector," different from the two other sectors of government/politics and the economy/markets, which includes volunteer and nonprofit institutions, churches, clubs, athletic teams, musical societies, and close-knit neighborhoods. Tocqueville thought that this civil society was much larger, more vigorous, and more important in America than in other countries, and that Americans were much more engaged in these sorts of volunteer civic activities. The importance of American civil society, of course, fits with the emphasis on limited government. Suspicious of government authority, Americans might naturally look to voluntary institutions like churches or charities for solutions to problems that markets don't solve. This civil society, indeed, might well provide much of the communitarian fabric that would hold the country together, in a way that neither governments nor markets would. The traditional importance of this civil society in America is one reason that some observers (e.g., Putnam 1995) are alarmed at indications that it is now weakening, that civic engagement is eroding, volunteerism is declining, and people are less involved in community and neighborhood activities than they once were. Scholars are currently engaged in a vigorous debate about whether that weakening has actually taken place, what might have caused it, and what the future holds.

But Tocqueville was struck particularly by the emphasis on social and political equality in America. Of course, the Declaration of Independence had proclaimed that "all men are created equal." Expanding on that theme, Tocqueville began his classic *Democracy in America* as follows:

> Amongst the novel objects that attracted my attention during my stay in the United States, nothing struck me more forcibly than the general equality of condition among the people. I readily discovered the prodigious influence which this primary fact exercises on the whole course of society; it gives a peculiar direction to public opinion, and a peculiar tenor to the laws; it imparts new maxims to the governing authorities, and peculiar habits to the governed. . . . It has no less empire over civil society than over the government; it creates opinions, gives birth to new sentiments, founds novel customs, and modifies whatever it does not produce. . . . This equality of condition is the fundamental fact from which all others seem to be derived, and the central point at which all my observations constantly terminated.

Tocqueville, of course, was affected by his times and his background. He was accustomed in Europe to societies in which people were born into their station in life, social and economic classes were more clearly marked, and upward mobility was much less possible. He was himself born into a high station in France and took social, economic, and political disparities to be natural. Contrast this background, even after the French Revolution, with the America he saw. European and American class structures and opportunities for advancement were quite strikingly different.

While Tocqueville was favorably impressed with the extent of equality he found in America, he was also cognizant of its dangers. In *Democracy in America*, he wrote with some eloquence about the possibility of a "tyranny of the majority" in America. His worry was that our insistence on equality would seriously erode the people's freedom and reverence for individualism. This erosion would come about, he argued, through the omnipotence of the majority. If people are equal, after all, then they settle disputes not by resort to authority or to expertise, but by taking a vote in which the majority rules. Whether the majority is right or informed doesn't matter; it's the majority. One could always argue against arbitrary authority such as a monarchy, Tocqueville thought, but one could not resist the moral authority of majority rule. The unfortunate consequence, he claimed, was a kind of sameness and disappearance of the very individualism Americans held so dear. "I know of no country," he said, "in which there is so little independence of mind and real freedom of discussion as in America." (See also Lipset 1979:106,137)

Tocqueville may have been only partially right. American equality, of course, did not extend to women and African Americans in the 1830s. Shklar (1991) points out, in fact, that slavery set up a fundamental contradiction to the principle of equality, the remnants of which have lasted to the present day. There were also obvious differences in the relative wealth of early Americans. Most of the founders enjoyed much more property and wealth than ordinary citizens did. Beyond that, Tocqueville's concern about a tyranny of the majority in America turned out to be rather controversial. The pluralism of the country and the incoherence of majorities for much of the time led Robert Dahl (1956) to argue more than a century after Tocqueville that, as a matter of fact, American politics was more like "minorities rule" rather than majority rule or minority rule.

Despite the obvious facts that the founders did not abolish slavery or bring women into full equality, Wood (1992) argues that the value the American Revolution placed on equality nevertheless set up the central justifications for subsequent successful efforts to free slaves, extend the franchise and other political and legal rights, and provide for greater economic and social mobility. Slavery, for instance, was simply incompatible with the intensely held principle of equality, and even though it took a long time, eventually that fundamental incompatibility brought about slavery's downfall. The founders' ideas thus had lasting power, well beyond their accomplishments in their own time, or even beyond their intentions. As Wood (1992:7–8) puts it, "The Revolution made possible the anti-slavery and women's rights movements of the nineteenth century and in fact all our current egalitarian thinking. The Revolution not only radically changed the personal and social relationships of people, . . . but also destroyed aristocracy as it had been understood in the Western world for at least two millennia."

To bring us back to our major task, that of comparing America to other advanced industrialized countries, it does seem that the class structure was less rigid, people were less firmly born into their station in life, and there was more occupational and geographical mobility in the United States than in other countries. Lipset (1977:103–110) argues that as systems have evolved over history, *actual* social mobility in the United States has come to be more similar to mobility in other countries than it was a couple of centuries ago, but that a big difference remains in the *value* that Americans place on equal opportunity and mobility. We don't need to demonstrate an American equality in some absolute idealized sense, or to argue that the country has no class, race, or other differences in wealth or power, to realize that in some respects (to be specified momentarily) the United States emphasizes equality more than other countries do.

There are different kinds of equality, however (see Rae 1981). Verba and Orren (1985), for instance, point out a difference between political and economic equality. Their analysis suggests that Americans are quite egalitarian in the political sphere, espousing the right to vote, free speech, and a disdain for aristocracy and privilege. But at the same time, Americans also tolerate and even prefer a great deal of inequality in the economic sphere, taking no particular exception to dramatic disparities in the incomes of rich and poor and opposing government programs designed to redistribute income. As Verba and Orren (1985:9) summarize the point, "Comparisons across a range of indicators reveal that the United States ranks among the most open and participatory of modern democracies when it comes to politics and among the least egalitarian when it comes to economic matters."

It has become common in the literature on equality to make a central distinction between *equality of result* and *equality of opportunity*. Americans apparently don't place much stock in equality of result. It is surely true that income disparities in the United States are extreme by comparison to other countries. In 1990, American households in the top decile of the income distribution had disposable incomes that were nearly six times greater than households in the bottom decile, compared to 4.0 in Canada, 3.8 in Britain, and 2.7 in Sweden (Topel 1997:55). When Burtless (1994:82) compared the overall poverty rate in the United States in the mid-1980s with the comparably calculated rates in six other industrialized countries, he concluded that the rate in the United States was the highest by far: 13.3 percent, followed by Canada, at 7.0 percent. The lowest rate among the seven was West Germany's 2.8 percent, while Sweden, France, Britain, and Australia ranged in between Germany and Canada. Much of the difference, according to Burtless, was due to the other countries' much more generous government programs affecting poverty: far longer-lasting unemployment benefits, children's allowances and subsidized child care centers, higher old-age and disability benefits, and guaranteed health insurance for their entire populations.

Disparities between rich and poor within the United States are also growing at a fast clip. Burtless (1996) shows that in 1969, income at the ninety-fifth percentile of adjusted personal income in the United States was a little less than twelve times income at the fifth percentile, while by 1993 it was more than twenty-five times as much. The very wealthy Americans, in other words, are very wealthy indeed, and far more wealthy than the poor. As far as equality of result is concerned, the American rich are far richer than the relatively poor, that disparity is growing, and it's much greater than it is in other industrialized countries.

Americans could look at such a huge inequality of result and find it politically and even morally repugnant. But while some do, most don't. It's part of American ideology to believe not that the rich should be whittled down to size, but rather that we can all aspire to be rich one day, or at least that our children can. So it isn't our impulse to even out financial or other resources. Lipset (1996:75–76) cites a good bit of survey evidence to the effect that Americans favor government programs designed to even out income, provide jobs, or help the unemployed much less than citizens of other industrialized countries do. McCloskey and Zaller (1984:82) summarize their survey data: "Most Americans strongly—even overwhelmingly— support the notion that everyone should have the same *chance* to 'get ahead,' but they are uniformly negative toward suggestions that everyone must end up with the same economic rewards."

While equality of *result* isn't the American goal, equality of *opportunity* is. As Huntington (1981:38) observes, "Equality in American thinking has rarely been interpreted as economic equality in terms of wealth and income, but rather as equality of opportunity." This is supposed to be the land of opportunity. Immigrants traveled to America in the first place to take advantage of the opportunities that they thought awaited them in the New World. So far as I can tell, the power of this notion of equality of opportunity is quite uniquely American. The idea is that the country doesn't need to provide for income equality or other kinds of equality of result. If it provides equality of opportunity, the center of American thinking goes, then if people don't do well, it's their own fault (Lipset 1979:174). They failed to take advantage of the opportunities they had.

It's not the case, however, that equality of opportunity actually exists in the United States. Indeed, a considerable body of writing (e.g., Haveman and Wolfe 1994) shows that life chances at birth are strikingly unequal, divided by class, race, gender, and other variables. That is, people born into poverty, people whose parents had a poor education, African Americans, women, and others are disadvantaged from birth; they don't in fact have the same opportunities. But we're talking not about the objective facts but about a prevailing American ideology that differs from the ideology of people who inhabit other industrialized countries. And the power of this notion of equality of opportunity, at least as an ideal, is distinctively American, at least in the sense that the American center of gravity is different from the center in other countries.

The logic of equality of opportunity also justifies the *in*equality of result noticeable in the United States. Relative poverty is seen to be the responsibility of the poor—they didn't take advantage of their opportunities. Isn't that an interesting twist? Many Americans can rationalize the tremendous income inequalities and the nagging presence of poverty by resorting to this concept of equality of opportunity. We can also rationalize our unwillingness to provide the sorts of ambitious government programs in such areas as health, welfare, and unemployment compensation that most other countries provide. If unfortunate people were regarded as the victims of forces beyond their control, or simply down on their luck, then we could see our way clear to having government provide for them: "There but for the grace of God go I." But if, in the land of opportunity, they're responsible for their own condition, then self-help rather than government help is the appropriate prescription. At most, government programs should be designed to enhance opportunity, but nothing more.

I'm not justifying this way of thinking about inequality of result and appropriate government remedies; I'm just describing it. Its validity does turn on the assumption that equality of opportunity in fact exists, which the research on life chances calls into question. But valid or not, I do think this intriguing reconciliation of inequality of result and equality of opportunity is part of what I'm calling the prevailing American ideology.

Vigorous debates are, of course, taking place both within the United States and within other countries about the validity of this notion of equality of opportunity. Some Americans do not agree with the prevailing notion that equality of opportunity justifies inequality of result, whereas some citizens of other countries do agree with it. But again, as I said at the outset of this chapter, I'm trying to describe the *center* in the United States, as compared with the center in other countries. It does seem that more Americans than others hold to the notion of equality of opportunity, which shifts the American debate to the right. One consequence could be that American social policies are less ambitious than those in other countries, and the American welfare state smaller. We'll have more to say about that connection between political thought and policy outcomes in a moment.

This notion of equality of opportunity also resolves an inherent tension between the values Americans place on individualism and on equality. If "equality" meant equality of result, then the value placed in equality would run directly counter to the value placed on individualism. After all, individualism implies the freedom of each person to achieve as much as he or she possibly can, which will inevitably result in disparities in financial or other attainments. That would indeed violate a principle of equality of result.

But if it means equality of opportunity rather than equality of result, then Americans can believe that successful individuals are simply the ones who achieved, based on the same opportunities as everyone else. They worked harder, were smarter, or had some other sort of advantage based on their individual merit. Wood (1969:71) points out that the American-style emphasis on equality of opportunity doesn't deny that some people turn out better than others. The difference, Wood argues, is that the inequality of result doesn't come from inherited wealth or social class.

Again, whether people actually do start on a level playing field is beside this particular point. In the prevailing American ideology, equality of opportunity is entirely compatible with individualism. So a concentration on opportunities rather than results resolves the inherent tension between the two central American values of individualism and equality.

A NOTE ON PUBLIC OPINION

Many of the arguments among scholars over whether there is a distinctive American political culture or a distinctive American ideology often involve analyses of public opinion data (e.g., Almond and Verba 1963). Scholars marshal survey evidence and study the general public in order to suggest that Americans value some things that Europeans don't value, or that American preferences about the appropriate role of government are or are not different from those of the citizens of other countries. I myself have referred to public opinion data in the pages you have just read. These disputes among scholars naturally raise the question of where political culture resides. If we want to characterize "Americans," *which* Americans should we study?

To make my position clear, if I were to look for the content of American ideology or American political culture, I probably wouldn't look only at the mass public. Or more precisely, I wouldn't rely on survey data of the general public as my only indicator of political culture or ideology. I would want to know quite a lot about elite political culture as well as mass political culture. Why?

The main reason for not looking only at the mass public to measure American ideology is that the thinking that matters for much of what we want to understand in this book is to be found elsewhere. If I had wanted to know about American ideology at the time of the founders, for instance, I wouldn't have relied solely on a public opinion survey, even if one had been available, because the ideology that mattered was the ideology held by the leaders who drafted the Constitution and argued for its adoption.

It's true that in a representative democracy such as ours, ideas in the mass public do affect election outcomes, and so do provide a kind of general constraint or direction to our institutions and public policies. People do have opinions, they act on their opinions (Page and Shapiro 1992), and legislators pay attention to their constituents' opinions (Jackson and King 1989; Kingdon 1989). In that sense, elections and the institutions of representative government do provide a specific mechanism by which popular values are related to public policies. Those popular values, however, are not always those of ordinary Americans (Kingdon 1989:Chs.2,12). The mass public constrains elected officials, but attentive and activist publics constrain them more tightly.

To study the prevailing American ideology, I'd prefer to look at the writings of Madison, for instance, or the speeches of contemporary elected leaders, at least as much as opinions in the mass public. Those are the folks who have prevailed, after all, and are responsible for the major directions that the country has taken in institutional design and in public policy. It's much more important that President Clinton declares in 1996 that "the era of big government is over" (whether it is or not) than that Joe Sixpack thinks so.

Indeed, McCloskey and Zaller (1984:234), clearly analysts of mass public opinion data, trace opinions in the mass public to opinions at the elite level: "When most opinion leaders agree on a given issue, the more politically sophisticated members of the general public tend to learn and adopt the elite norm as their own. When they disagree, however, the members of the public who are politically aware begin to divide in ways that mirror the disagreements among the opinion leaders." So the elite level affects the mass level as much as, or perhaps even more than, the other way around.

Nevertheless, survey data exist on some of the topics we have been discussing that can supply additional information on American ideas. In a very general sense, those survey data bear out the description of American ideology that I have presented here: a distinctive belief in limited government. One study (reported in Heidenheimer et al. 1983:321) asked respondents in several countries how much responsibility they thought government should have in education, health care, housing, old age security, and employment. Popular support for government action in all of these areas was lowest in the United States. When other surveys, conducted in forty-three countries, asked people whether there should be more government ownership of business and industry or more private ownership, the United States was the world's leader in favoring private over government ownership (Inglehart 1997:263). Lipset (1996) marshals public opinion data that compare preferences and values in various countries to show that Americans distinctively favor freedom to develop without hindrance, as opposed to equality of income (p 72); oppose government policies designed to redistribute wealth (pp 72–73); favor freedom over equality (pp 101, 145); favor financial rewards for reliability, hard work, and efficiency (p 144); and favor government programs to promote equality of opportunity, but not equality of result (p 145).

In fairness, the picture isn't completely one-sided. There is some survey evidence, for instance, that the American public would prefer an increasing government role in health care, and even some sort of comprehensive national health insurance (Steinmo and Watts 1995:332). Both Steinmo and Watts (1995) and King (1973) argue that Americans prefer the extension of existing social services and the establishment of new ones at about the same rate as citizens of other countries. Their point is that public policies seem to be neither a simple translation of public preferences into government actions nor a governmental response to public demand; if they were, U.S. policies would not look so different from those of other countries. But as Free and Cantril (1967:36) show, this approval of government programs clashes with people's ideology of distrust of government, resulting in Americans as "operational liberals, ideological conservatives." There is a difference between preferences and culture, in other words, a point to which I return below. In addition, Stimson (1991) shows that public opinion shifts a good bit from one time to another, as opposed to exhibiting lasting cultural verities.

Some of these arguments simply reinforce the position that the mass public is not the only place to find political culture, and that survey evidence may not tell the whole story. After all, if we're speaking of *political* culture, the place to find it is among people who are political (White 1995b). Beyond that point, it's difficult to interpret surveys in which people say they favor some proposal. In response to questions, people favor many things, and it's not entirely clear how they themselves would translate those preferences into policies. They may favor national health insurance in the abstract, for instance, but still be quite responsive to arguments against a "big government takeover of health care" (White 1995b). To cite another example (Steinmo 1993:17), people are charmingly prepared to favor lower taxes, increased government benefits, and a balanced budget all at the same time.

Recognizing the ambiguities and even contradictions in the public opinion data, it's still fair to conclude that public opinion is very roughly consistent with the characterization of American ideology I have set forth. Americans, more than citizens of other industrialized countries, favor limited government and stress individual advancement over collective purposes. When it comes to equality, Americans distinctively favor equality of opportunity, but not equality of result. We found these themes strikingly true in our discussion of individualism and equality, and not substantially contradicted in the opinions of the mass public. Again, it's important to emphasize that we're making comparisons among countries here, not trying to assess American values and preferences in relation to some abstract ideal. Americans need not be "essentially" or "uniformly" individualistic, for instance, but only "relatively" so compared to citizens of other industrialized countries.

Page and Shapiro (1992:118) present one rather good summary of the state of American public opinion, which captures both this emphasis on individualism and the emphasis on equality of opportunity. After going through a number of survey findings that show rather stable opinions on economic welfare issues over the years since the 1930s, they state:

> This configuration of preferences reflects a fundamental individualism that esteems individual responsibility and individual initiative, and relies primarily upon free enterprise capitalism for economic production and distribution. Yet it also reflects a sense of societal obligation, a

strong commitment to government action in order to
smooth capitalism's rough edges, to regulate its excesses,
to protect the helpless, and to provide a substantial
degree of equal opportunity for all.

The extent to which and, more important, the *ways* in which the values
and preferences of ordinary citizens matter is of course another question.
For instance, Page and Shapiro (1992:117) show that at the height of the
deregulation movement in public policy in the 1970s and 1980s, there was
very little public support for deregulation. So public policy is not made by
some simple translation of popular preferences into government action.
Rather, the public sets fairly broad constraints on government action,
within which policymakers have considerable discretion (Kingdon
1989:68,288). We will return to that question at the end of this chapter,
when we try to sort through the swirl of arguments among scholars about
the importance of institutions, as opposed to the importance of culture or
ideology.

SOME RESULTS OF
AMERICAN IDEOLOGY

We have argued that Americans think about the proper role of government
in a distinctive way. If Americans hold on to the tenets of this prevailing
ideology, then that ideology affects the differences between the United
States and other industrialized countries described in Chapter 2. So let's
think about the consequences of American ideology for the structure of
the nation's governmental institutions, the strength of its political parties,
and the shape of its public policies.

INSTITUTIONS

The prevailing American ideology I have just described starts with the
impulse to limit government. That impulse left a completely clear mark on
American governmental institutions. In their desire to combat the evils of
faction and guard against government tyranny, the founders deliberately
erected a governmental structure that would make government action difficult. The separation of powers, checks and balances, a bicameral Congress, and a federal system were all designed to ensure that no one faction
could capture power, and that mobilizing this cumbersome apparatus for
action would be extremely difficult. The design of an independent judiciary, furthermore, provided another check on government action
(Skowronek 1982) and added a protection for minorities against majorities
(Casper 1976). The founders' philosophy of government thus clearly
affected the institutions they designed. And that philosophy, emphasizing

as it does the desirability and necessity of limiting government, very much conforms to the features of the prevailing American ideology I have just described.

It's possible, of course, that the founders' ideology didn't translate into their governmental design. Instead, they could have adopted their chosen design for some other reasons, and arguments such as those in *The Federalist* could have been rationalizations. But as I have argued elsewhere (Kingdon 1993), a given communicator's words tell us a lot about the world around that communicator. The words are constructed to appeal to an audience, and the writer builds arguments on the values of that audience in order to persuade them. Even if the writers of *The Federalist,* for instance, did not really hold to the ideas they enunciated (a remote possibility, to my mind), their essays still reflect the ideas of the larger set of people to whom they were appealing. Thus it is likely that the rhetoric of limited government struck a responsive chord in the attentive public of the time.

POLITICAL PARTIES

Let's think for a moment about what broad-based, large political parties do. Fundamentally, parties mobilize majorities for elections and organize for government action when in office. Interest groups represent narrower, sometimes extremely narrow, interests. But political parties aggregate those interests together into diverse coalitions, with the aim of capturing a majority of votes in elections. That's most obviously true in two-party systems in which one of the two parties becomes a governing majority. But even in multiparty systems where elections are based on proportional representation, in which each party may represent a minority of the electorate, a majority coalition in the parliament must still be constructed. Thus strong political parties would have the potential for bridging the separation of powers and federalism, and for mobilizing even fragmented government institutions for action.

This aggregative character of political parties runs squarely counter to the traditional American emphasis on individualism and autonomy. Americans seem to want to avoid subordinating individual rights and privileges to some sort of collective organization like a party. That's one reason the American system of representation emphasizes the autonomous individual legislator, responsive to and accountable to his or her own constituents rather than to party leadership. Most of my American students, for instance, find it very odd that parliamentarians in other countries vote in lockstep with their party leadership. We Americans prize the fragmentation and decentralization we have constructed; and we're suspicious of aggregation or collectivization.

The Progressives set about to weaken political parties early in the twentieth century. I described in the last chapter the measures that weakened parties, including the use of direct primaries rather than caucuses of party activists to nominate candidates, and the erosion of patronage as a serious party-maintaining mechanism. The Progressives' dual commitments to broader democratic participation through such devices as the direct primary and the ballot initiative on the one hand and to decision making by experts through such devices as regulatory agencies and a professional civil service on the other are often seen as antithetical. But Balogh (1991) argues that both themes were attacks on well-organized and well-financed interests that the Progressives thought were plundering the country, such as corporations, railroads, trusts, monopolies, and corrupt political parties.

There was nothing inevitable or predetermined about the Progressive era, and no Hartzian liberal consensus guided the outcomes. Progressive reforms were not enacted without tremendous battles over a long period of time, and they were instituted only partially. Skowronek (1982) shows, for instance, that the expansion of administrative capacities favored by the Progressives was actually something of a jerry-built patchwork compared to the administrative states of Europe. As Balogh (1991:144) puts it, "The resistance of politicians wedded to a more decentralized and partisan system of politics combined with the pervasiveness of the antistatist strain in American political culture severely restricted the development of federal administrative mechanisms."

There is some doubt, as I said in the last chapter, about whether the weakening of parties was the main aim of the Progressives or a by-product of their attack on privilege and corruption. Either way, weaker parties meant an erosion in the ability to aggregate interests and to mobilize government to action. And either way, the reforms were also closely linked to what I have described the prevailing ideology at the center of American politics. The Progressive reform proposals, in other words, fell on the fertile ground of American suspicion of the concentration of wealth and power. If Americans prize individualism, autonomy, and decentralization more than other countries do, then it makes perfect sense to attack arrangements that centralize and aggregate. Since parties do those things, therefore, it makes sense to weaken them.

We will have more to say about the genesis of movements to weaken political parties, including the assault on urban machines, in the next chapter.

PUBLIC POLICY

The American emphasis on individualism and limited government has obvious direct consequences for the shape of our public policies. As King (1973:418) puts it, "The State plays a more limited role in America than elsewhere because Americans, more than other people, want it to play a limited role."

First, Americans don't tolerate taxes very well. Citizens of other industrialized countries complain about taxes, of course. But their attitude seems quite different. They seem to realize that government is supposed to provide for certain collective purposes and that taxes are the inevitable accompaniment of those implicit collective decisions. If they decide that government should finance national health insurance and passenger rail service, for instance, then they regard raising the revenue to accomplish those ends through taxation as the logical consequence of such a decision.

We Americans, by contrast, seem to see taxes as devices for confiscating what is rightfully ours. As fiercely autonomous individuals, we believe we are entitled to our wealth, and that taxes take away the wealth that it is our natural right to obtain and keep. This country was born in the aftermath of the Boston Tea Party, after all, a classic protest against taxes. And this attitude toward taxation has lasted right down to the taxpayer revolts that have swept across the country in the last couple of decades.

Recollect, for example, what has happened to recent presidential candidates or presidents who have even hinted that raising taxes would be part of the way to eliminate the federal budget deficit. Walter Mondale told the 1984 electorate that he would raise taxes, apparently thinking that voters would reward him for his honesty, and was crushingly defeated. George Bush told the electorate in 1988 to "read my lips—no new taxes," and was elected. Then he agreed to tax increases in the budget compromise of 1990. His dramatic words about lipreading came back to haunt him in the election of 1992, when Pat Buchanan replayed Bush's videotaped pledge in primary after primary, mortally wounding his general election candidacy. Bill Clinton's deficit reduction in 1993 included tax increases, particularly on the most wealthy individuals. He was rewarded in the congressional election of 1994 with the first Republican-controlled House of Representatives in forty years, and subsequently wondered out loud about whether the tax increases had been a good idea. Although each of these election results were due to multiple causes, of which tax policy was only one, the lesson from this recent experience still seems hard to escape: Don't raise taxes. Don't even think of raising taxes. Certainly don't think out loud about it. And if you must do it, figure out a way to hide it.

Beyond taxes, in Chapter 2 I described many areas of public policy in which American government programs are much less ambitious than those of other industrialized countries. Our programs in health, welfare, housing, transportation, and many other areas are much smaller and less ambitious. And the public sector as a proportion of GDP is noticeably smaller.

This general pattern of public policy is a direct result of the American ideology of limited government described above. Americans see many areas as private that citizens of other countries see as public. People in country after country think of various activities as "naturally" a public or governmental responsibility that Americans think of "naturally" as something that private individuals should provide for. King (1973:418) summarizes these American beliefs as a series of what he calls "catch phrases: free enterprise is more efficient than government; governments should concentrate on encouraging private initiative and free competition; government is wasteful; governments should not provide people with things they can provide for themselves; too much government endangers liberty; and so on."

Take health insurance as an example. All other industrialized countries have some version of national health insurance that covers the entire population (White 1995a). It may be financed directly by taxes or indirectly by employer mandates, but government does enact policies that provide for universal health insurance coverage. In the United States, by contrast, many people purchase health insurance privately or get it as a fringe benefit from their employer, government fills in some of the gaps with programs for the poor (Medicaid) and the elderly (Medicare), but some of the population is left uncovered. Even the first Clinton administration's ill-starred health care proposal, which its opponents portrayed as the essence of big government, relied on an elaborate system of purchasing alliances in order to *avoid* setting up a direct government program. President Richard Nixon once defended his health care proposal, which relied on employer mandates, by saying that government-run national health insurance wasn't "the American way." Indeed.

Scholars sometimes argue that a theory that attributes a given American public policy to a general feature of the American political culture misses the distinctive properties of that particular policy arena. According to this view, a theory that attributes the absence of national health insurance to the general American distrust of government, for instance, misses the importance of the particular configuration of interest groups involved in health care policy. But in a way, that's the point. This pattern of limited government policies, compared to other countries, is so common across so many policy arenas that there must be something larger at work than the politics and economics of any single arena.

So the prevailing American ideology of limited government ties in quite directly to smaller, less ambitious government policies in area after area. But what mechanisms tie ideology to policy? A major link between this ideology and public policy is the mechanism of elections, because elections imply both the importance of mass, attentive, and activist publics and the need for politicians to appeal to those publics for support. Those appeals, my argument runs, are particularly successful in America when they strike the chords of limited government and individualism, which resonate more strongly in America than in other countries. Thus the pattern of public policy is closely linked to the way we think about the proper role of government.

"EXCEPTIONS" TO THE POLICY PATTERN

In Chapter 2, we noticed some supposed exceptions to the general pattern of limited public policies. Public education, for instance, enjoys a much firmer and more long-standing tradition in the United States than in other industrialized countries. American government regulation in some areas seems to be more intrusive than in other countries. America is comparatively litigious, and the criminal justice system is more far-reaching. The U.S. military establishment is large. It is time now to explain those exceptions in terms of American ideology.

A few pages back, I highlighted the distinctive American concept of equality of *opportunity*, as opposed to equality of *result*. America doesn't strive for greater equality in incomes, for example, and doesn't insist that government provide equal services to everybody. But Americans, partly because they think of this country as "the land of opportunity," are willing and even eager for government to provide for equal opportunity. If people are given opportunity, the central thinking goes, and then don't get ahead, it's their own fault and not the responsibility of government to rectify.

That concept of equality of opportunity explains Americans' distinctive support for public education (King 1973:420). The United States is a world leader in government (federal, state, and local) support for schools at elementary, secondary, and university levels. Education doesn't necessarily level incomes or status, but it does supposedly provide the skills and knowledge that people need to take advantage of opportunities. That's why Americans make an exception to their usual opposition to big government for education. When I was interviewing members of Congress in an earlier piece of research (Kingdon 1989), I was struck by the extent to which even the most conservative, rock-ribbed, antigovernment Republicans were willing to make an exception for education. Education provides for opportunity, the thinking goes, and people are usually willing to pay the price in taxes for this purpose. Whether education actually does make opportunities equal or whether America actually is the land of opportunity might be factually in dispute. But the package of ideas that make up the prevailing American ideology, which includes the concept of equality of opportunity, is very much related to the supposed "exception" of support for government-operated public education.

Equality of opportunity is also related to other policy areas in sometimes subtle ways. Heclo (1986:321) argues that the Great Society programs in the 1960s, including Medicare, Medicaid, aid to education, and the poverty program, were "wrapped up in a concept of *opportunity* for the disadvantaged that seemed fully in tune with the American political philosophy." He goes on to emphasize the significance of what did *not* happen, as well as what did happen: "By way of contrast, there was little inclination at that time on anyone's part to take on the much more politically difficult task of selling the American people on a major program of social reconstruction and income redistribution." Thus does this unusual combination of opportunity with individualism in American ideology guide poverty policy, and many other policy areas as well. Affirmative action, for instance, whether you support it or oppose it, is intended to further equality of opportunity.

Let's turn to regulation, another seeming exception to Americans' opposition to intrusive government. The apparent greater American government regulation of some aspects of private activity, which seems paradoxical, is actually related to the prevailing ideology in some interesting ways. We noticed that individualism prompts Americans to object to taxation and to resist the expensive government programs that are the norm in other industrialized countries. That drive to keep government small paradoxically sometimes prompts vigorous government regulation. It works this way: In other countries, when faced with a given problem, the impulse is to create a government program to deal with it—a program that spends public money and raises it through taxation. In the United States, the impulse is to leave the activity in the private sector, but then to regulate it, either by government regulation or by private rights of action in court. Thus Americans regulate instead of tax. Fuel consumption, for instance, is discouraged by creating a federal system of corporate average fuel economy standards or mandating electric cars in California—regulatory devices—rather than by raising gasoline taxes sharply (Nivola and Crandall 1995).

That same dynamic leads to American litigiousness, which turns out to be a form of social regulation through private actions in court. We noticed earlier that lawyers and courts do things in America that bureaucrats do in other countries (Kagan and Axelrad 1997). As Nivola (1997:25) puts it, "Americans may be trading lower levels of government interference and direct taxation for a greater frequency of costly civil actions." Instead of having government agencies forcing businesses to protect consumers or employees in various ways, for instance, consumers or employees are allowed to bring suit in court. To take another example, government agencies don't drum incompetent doctors out of their practices; aggrieved patients bring malpractice suits instead. Environmental regulation is sometimes accomplished in the United States by passing laws that give individuals the right to bring suit in court against polluters, or give polluters the right to sue others to contribute to cleanup costs. Accident and injury victims are reimbursed in many other countries through publicly financed compensation funds; in the United States, they sue. Instead of treating issues such as health or welfare as matters of social insurance, as they are in many other countries, Americans treat them as individual rights. Thus resources that could be spent simply on insurance are spent instead on litigation (Kagan and Axelrad 1997). Other countries often provide government subsidies to employers to hire and retain disabled workers; the United States offers such workers recourse to the courts instead (Burke 1997). The whole phenomenon of class action suits in America's tort litigation system is a way to accomplish in court what other countries often achieve by bureaucratic regulation. The legal systems of many other countries, furthermore, do not allow contingency fees, thus sharply reducing incentives for lawyers to represent aggrieved parties in negligence suits.

Nivola (1997) provides many examples of this American pattern of accomplishing social regulation through litigation, which springs from laws that grant private rights of action, rather than through action by government bureaucracies.

This tendency is directly related to the distinctive American avoidance of government programs that this book has already examined. In line with American individualism, we provide for individuals to take action by hiring a lawyer and bringing suit. And consistent with American distrust of government, we encourage remedies through the courts rather than through government programs administered by executive branch agencies. Little wonder that we end up with an abundance of lawyers.

Kagan (1991) calls this a system of "adversarial legalism." Kagan and Axelrad (1997:154–55) argue that adversarial legalism

> is not an arbitrary choice. It reflects a political tradition that from the nation's beginnings harbored antipathy for hierarchically organized, concentrated government power. . . . The demands for an activist agenda are channeled through governmental and economic structures that reflect the traditional mistrust of concentrated power and a reluctance to pay the high taxes that support European-style bureaucracies and welfare programs. . . . Lawsuits, rights, penalties, lawyers, courts, and juries thus are the U.S. substitutes for the powerful central bureaucracies, corporatist bodies, central banks, and keiretsu that dominate the social regulatory regimes of other advanced democracies.

Nor is the importance of courts and litigation a recent development. Skowronek (1982) points to the strength of courts and the weakness of bureaucracy in nineteenth-century America. He shows that a version of an American administrative state was created in the early part of the twentieth century, but obviously court power and bureaucratic weakness remain.

There is a good bit of writing these days about America as a "litigious society." We noticed in Chapter 2, indeed, that the United States has more lawyers per capita and more tort litigation costs as a percentage of GDP than any other industrialized country, and by a wide margin. But the preceding analysis suggests that American litigiousness is not simply a straightforwardly cultural trait. Instead, it is clearly related to deliberate public policy decisions that have been made at all levels of government. As a part of our distinctive prevailing ideology, Americans at the political center tend to oppose taxation, distrust bureaucracy, and eschew "big government," more than people at the political center of other countries do. Thus in order to accomplish certain social objectives in this country, public policies provide for people to go to court instead of establishing the government subsidies or programs that other countries have. Litigiousness is related to American ideology, all right, but via this rather subtle route of affecting public policies through deliberate choices made in the context of governmental institutions, instead of being the direct cultural effect, as is often assumed. And as for solutions to the tremendous cost of litigation in the United States, as Kagan and Axelrad (1997:181) say, "Curbing adversarial legalism may not always be easy to reconcile with a quest for smaller government," because governmental programs, subsidies, and regulation would be required to achieve many of the objectives that litigation supposedly seeks.

To turn to another "exception," even the comparatively high levels of crime and incarceration in the United States may be related to American ideology, albeit in an odd way. Lipset (1991:31) claims that the crime rate is related to the emphasis on individualism and opportunity. Since, as the mythology goes, America is a land of opportunity in which individuals' paths to success supposedly aren't blocked by class barriers or artificial economic structures, then economic failure is seen more as the individual's fault than is the case in cultures that emphasize barriers to advancement (e.g., unalterable class or social station), which are beyond the individual's control. If you're unemployed, for instance, Americans see your situation more as your own fault and less due to economic cycles or structures beyond your control than people in other countries do. This view affects American orientation toward many public policies, as we have seen. There is willingness to provide for opportunity, for instance, but not for income redistribution as a way of combating poverty.

But oddly enough, this thinking might also be related to a resort to crime. Crime is another way, Lipset speculates, albeit an unconventional and illegal way, to seize your opportunities in the land of opportunity, and to achieve the individual financial success that Americans prize. Beyond that, I would add, some expressions of individualism can be more heavily regulated in other countries than in the United States. Great Britain, for instance, simply banned private ownership of handguns in 1997, an unthinkable government action in this country. American gun owners' insistence that their constitutional right to bear arms extends to handguns, from this perspective, is simply an extension of a more general American insistence on individual rights, albeit taken to an extreme in terms of cross-national comparison.

We also noted in Chapter 2 that American governments criminalize some activities that are not treated as criminal in many other countries. Smoking is now banned in public places across the country, for instance; prostitution is illegal in most localities; American speed limits are lower than they are in France or Germany, and speed traps are unknown in some countries; gambling is much more strictly regulated than in Britain; some states' sodomy laws criminalize homosexual contact between consenting adults; and so on. This criminalization of more activities obviously leads to more offenses. These sorts of government regulation do not seem to square entirely with the emphasis on individualism that I have been discussing. But it's possible that this American tendency springs from another theme in American political life, a distinctive strand of moralism which may be related to the early importance of Protestant sects, which we will discuss in the next chapter. This point is obviously speculative, but it could be that this moral code frowns on and even criminalizes activities that in other countries would be legal and even acceptable.

Our final "exception" is national defense. We noted in Chapter 2 that the United States has a much larger military establishment than an ideology of limited government would dictate. Part of the explanation, of course, may have little to do with American ideology. Superpower status has its costs, for example, and the United States has been thrust into a position of international leadership during this century. But some of the explanation may be related to American ideas. A considerable part of the justification for a larger defense establishment in the second half of the twentieth century was the Cold War, and the threat that communism posed to American interests. Communism was seen not only as a threat to American business interests but also as a threat to "the American way" or to American ideas. Of course there was a pork-barrel aspect to defense spending, as localities and industries benefited from procurement, bases, and the like. But pork itself could be provided in other ways, like mass transit and other government spending. So why this way? I think defense spending was related to anticommunism, which in turn was very much bound up in the prevailing American ideology. From that point of view, it's no accident that defense spending has been declining as a porportion of the federal budget since the end of the cold war—we don't see the same threat.

INSTITUTIONS AND IDEAS

Scholars are engaged in a lively discussion about the relative importance of institutions and ideas in determining the patterns of a country's public policies. One can classify some writers in the "cultural" or "idea-based" camp. To these scholars, the major source of national differences in public policy is the differences in the countries' philosophies of government. In a country like the United States, they argue, there is simply a great skepticism about government and a high value placed on limiting government. Other scholars are in the "institutional" camp. They don't believe that differences in political culture explain public policy outcomes very well and point instead to the consequences of institutional arrangements. They see parliamentary governments as more capable of being mobilized for action than governments based on separation of powers, for instance.

One "idea-based" scholar is King (1973), who begins by describing the differences between the public policies of the United States and those of other countries and noting that, with a few exceptions such as public education, America is distinctive in its smaller government and less ambitious public policies. He then goes through a number of possible explanations for that distinctiveness, discarding each in turn. With regard to institutions, despite the fact that American institutions—separation of powers, checks and balances, bicameralism, federalism, weak political parties, and powerful courts—are unwieldy, King still argues that American government is fully capable of mobilizing for action if the situation warrants it. Indeed, it has done so, as the case of governmental responses to the Great Depression in the 1930s shows. In other words, institutional barriers to action can be overcome, and the differences between the United States and other industrialized countries must lie in the different ideas that dominate their respective politics. In this country the option of ambitious government programs, in one policy arena after another, tends either not to arise or not to be taken seriously in the first place. During the New Deal period of the 1930s, for instance, Franklin Roosevelt did not propose comprehensive national health insurance, as King points out, and America considered only health insurance for the elderly and poor in the 1960s. The institutional weaknesses and barriers could be overcome, King argues, if such options were on the table, but Americans don't take these options seriously because they hold to a philosophy of limited government.

A number of other scholars fall into this "culturalist" or "idea-based" category. Although the following capsule description oversimplifies his writing somewhat, Lipset (1979, 1996) stresses the importance of overarching American values, such as individualism, laissez faire, and equality of opportunity. Huntington (1981) speaks of an "American Creed," which emphasizes some of the same values. Inglehart (1997) compares values in many countries, describing differences among countries and changes over time. And much of this chapter has stressed the prevailing themes in American culture and American political thought.

Other writers who compare public policies across countries are quite skeptical about explanations for the policy differences among countries that concentrate on differences in culture, ideology, values, or prevailing philosophies. Steinmo (1994:106), for instance, although agreeing that "the rhetoric and symbolism of individualism is particularly strong in America," still concludes that "the most common and obvious explanation for America's exceptionally small state—that we have a uniquely individualistic political culture—is wrong." He thinks that a cultural explanation cannot account for change over time, that the culture contains contrasting elements that therefore can't guide public policy decisions very well, and that the causal mechanisms that would link culture to policy aren't at all clear.

Instead, Steinmo argues, American public policy is different because the country's extraordinarily fragmented governmental institutions, including the separation of powers and federalism, favor some interests and strategies and discourage others. In particular, his argument continues, fragmentation advantages those who seek to block proposals for ambitious government programs, because they need only block them at one point in the structure, whereas advocates must jump all of the hurdles (e.g., House, Senate, president, Supreme Court). Steinmo (1994:126) characterizes the American system as a "polity replete with veto points," and speculates that American public policy would look very much more ambitious if Franklin Roosevelt had been prime minister in a parliamentary system in the 1930s instead of the American president. Another institutional feature, strong political parties, could conceivably overcome some of the governmental fragmentation, but America also set about to weaken parties. Then fragmentation, relatively low funding levels, and lack of comprehensive approaches strip government of its efficacy, so that people are reinforced in their view that government can't get anything right: "When American governments do act, they too often act badly." (Steinmo 1994:106)

Debates over national health insurance, according to the institutionalists, illustrate the point. Steinmo and Watts (1995), in trying to understand why the United States has not adopted national health insurance despite frequent attempts over a century, argue that Americans want it as much as residents of other countries. The explanation for the difference, in other words, does not lie in Americans' ideology or ideas. Their explanation turns on such institutional barriers to action as the separation of powers, bicameralism, and federalism. The founders designed institutions to pit factions against each other and stifle majorities, and the Progressives added to the bias toward inaction by weakening political parties. Because America has erected these barriers, according to Steinmo and Watts, powerful interest groups like organized medicine, small business lobbies, and insurance companies are in a much better position to block action than such groups are in countries with more mobilizable government institutions. In their view, demands from the public and the configuration of interest groups are quite similar across the industrialized world. What is different is the institutions. In the words of their article's title, "It's the institutions, stupid!"

A number of other writers fall, roughly speaking, into this "institutionalist" camp. Weaver and Rockman (1993) ask the question, "Do institutions matter?" While they trace in complicated detail the conditions under which and the ways in which institutions matter, their answer is basically, "yes". Weir (1992a) argues that the fluidity of institutions makes America more receptive to new ideas than other countries might be, but the weakness of political parties and bureaucracies results in an inability to construct coalitions that would unite politics, ideas, and administration. Heclo (1986:332) too is skeptical of the notion that American public policy is formed by a distinctive American culture that emphasizes individualism and antistatism. He notes that the United States has actually provided for a considerable edifice of income transfers, wealth redistributions, and social programs of various kinds, and concludes, "These are not the signs of a people seized by rugged individualism. There must be more to the story than the intellectual hammerhold of John Locke."

I personally don't find it necessary to choose between institutional and cultural explanations for cross-national differences in public policy. Indeed, the really powerful explanation stresses the *combination* of ideas and institutions. As White (1995b:373) puts it, "Is it 'the institutions, stupid?' or the preferences of those who run them? Phrased that way, we all know that both are implicated." Or to quote Smith (1995:387), "Institutions matter, but so do ideas, policy legacies, and key political interests."

To take the American case, the institutions didn't just spontaneously descend on the society and culture from afar. As I have argued earlier in this book, and as Steinmo and Watts acknowledge, the institutions arose from an ideological milieu. The founders held to an ideology that stressed the primacy of individual freedom and a profound distrust of government. Given that ideology, they designed the institutions to limit government and hamstring anybody's efforts to mobilize it to action. The weakening of political parties, as I argued above, reinforced limited government by weakening the major type of institution (parties) that would be capable of mobilizing for government action. So the institutions were intimately related to American ideology, and in no sense a kind of alternative explanation for subsequent events. Institutions and ideologies go together.

One problem with many critiques of cultural explanations for difference in public policies is that they measure culture by looking at contemporary popular preferences, as measured by survey research data. I noted earlier in this chapter that I wouldn't look to the mass public as my sole indicator of political culture. To expand on that point, political culture or systemic values are not the same as distributions of public preferences. Political culture includes, for instance, a set of central symbols to which advocates can appeal. Such symbols are not always reflected in survey questions designed to measure people's preferences about public policies. While the majority of Americans may prefer national health insurance when asked about it in a survey, for instance, they also respond to appeals to such distinctive symbols as government incompetence or tyranny, individual autonomy and supremacy, and limited government. Free and Cantril (1967:179) present convincing survey evidence that Americans express preferences for government programs providing education, health, old age benefits, jobs, and welfare, while at the same time they "cling to the traditional American ideology, which advocates the curbing of government power on social and domestic economic matters." Then elite-level opponents of proposals like national health insurance successfully appeal to those symbols, effectively sidestepping the distributions of preferences. No matter what type of national health care initiative Bill Clinton might have proposed, for instance, opponents were sure to attack it as "big government."

So we need to understand both elite and mass political ideologies. To understand political culture fully, we must know about the ideology of the founders, the ideas that motivated Progressives and other reformers, the values of contemporary government officials and other activists, and the ways in which elite-level ideas are passed along to the mass public. Beyond that, we need to understand the power of culture, including the powerful symbols to which elites appeal, as opposed to distributions of preferences in the mass public. Finally, elections are a major institutional mechanism that ties culture to policy; as I noted above, elected politicians react to, play on, and shape the ideas and cultural symbols that resonate with their constituents.

It's also important to remind ourselves one more time that we're trying to understand America in relation to other industrialized countries, not America in relation to some sort of ideological ideal. Heclo is quite right to take note of the fact that Americans have indeed built a version of a social welfare state, as have all other industrialized democracies. But the question we're trying to answer in the pages of this book is why the American version, in policy after policy, is with few exceptions less ambitious than that of other countries. To that comparative question, it seems to me, the existence of distinctive American values constitutes at least a partial answer.

One way to phrase my resolution of this seeming conflict in the literature over institutional versus idea-based explanations is to say that early American ideas affected institutional design. Then, once they were in place, the institutions proved to be quite sticky and quite difficult to change, as institutions always are. Such subsequent events as reforms designed to weaken political parties and the failure of a viable democratic socialist party to emerge reinforced this early start. So the institutions took on a life of their own. I emphatically do not mean that a consensus on the tenets of an American ideology set us down this path and that the whole of American history has been a kind of automatic playing out of our beginnings. To the contrary, there has been a lot of change, and history is replete with struggles over our ideas and directions at every turn. But the power of these institutions, rooted as they were in the founders' ideas and reinforced since by the prevailing American ideology at the center of our politics, is also evident at every turn. I elaborate on this line of argument with a story of "path dependence" at the end of Chapter 4.

Ideas have affected institutions. And American institutions in turn have affected ideology. Steinmo (1993:7) says, "The structure of a polity's decision-making institutions profoundly affects how interest groups, politicians, and bureaucrats develop their policy preferences." As Americans became accustomed to arrangements like the separation of powers, bicameralism, and federalism, they came to expect rather little of government in comparison with citizens of other countries. After all, the founders had deliberately constructed these governmental institutions so that they wouldn't work very smoothly. As the founders intended, American government is unwieldy, inefficient, and limited. Little wonder that Americans were reinforced in the view that government doesn't work well.

Actually, a close reading of both the "idea-based" and the "institutional" writers reveals that each side in the scholarly dispute grants part of the case of the other. Both sides say that their chosen emphasis, be it institutions or ideas, isn't the whole explanation for public policies. King knows that American institutions are unwieldy and capable of capture by intransigent interest groups; Steinmo knows that values are important, and that institutions don't produce their effects in isolation from the ideological context in which they were designed and are embedded. As Steinmo (1993:201) puts it: "Neither institutions nor values nor economic interests for that matter by themselves provide adequate explanations for significant political outcomes over time; these variables interact with one another and, in so doing, change with time." Skocpol (1985:20) makes the same point, stressing a two-way relationship between state and society: "Studies of states alone are not to be substituted for concerns with classes or groups; nor are purely state-determinist arguments to be fashioned in the place of society-centered explanations."

Institutions and ideology, therefore, affect each other. American governmental institutions sprang from a belief in limited government. Their subsequent performance reinforced that very belief. And the powerful *interaction* between institutions and ideology has affected the pattern of American public policy right from the beginning down to the present day.

CONCLUSION

This chapter has described a prevailing American ideology, which emphasizes individualism and a belief in limited government. I have argued that this ideology has resulted in the patterns, described in Chapter 2, that distinguish the United States from other industrialized countries: fragmented governmental institutions, weaker political parties, lower taxes, a smaller public sector relative to the size of our economy, and less ambitious and far-reaching government programs in most public policy areas. We have also traced the seeming "exceptions" in the usual pattern of limited government to the workings of this prevailing American ideology. We attributed the distinctive American support for public education, for instance, to the value that Americans place on equality of opportunity.

Not all Americans subscribe to this ideology. Critics from both the left and the right assail its tenets. It clearly does not represent a sort of American consensus or hegemony. Despite a wide diversity of opinion, however, I believe it is still possible to think of a center of gravity in American politics, and in the politics of other countries. The major point is that, in the main, the center in American politics is considerably to the right of the center in the politics of other industrialized countries. Furthermore, despite swings of the pendulum over time from left to right and back again, and despite the growth of government over this century, the United States has remained different from other countries over most of its history. So these ideas are both stable and distinctive in this comparative sense.

Again, I'm not justifying this distinctively American orientation toward government. Some Americans admire it and believe that there is a continuing American genius evident in the thinking of the founders. Other Americans disagree with this orientation, some arguing that there is too much suspicion of government and too much reluctance to use government for collective purposes, others claiming that government even in the United States is too big and intrusive. Readers of this book are entitled to their own opinions about whether the current situation is desirable, and if undesirable, in what direction and by how much we should change. I will add some of my own opinions in the last chapter. But my main purpose at this point in the book is more modest: to describe the state of affairs as it factually is, and to understand why America is so different from other industrialized countries.

So far, we have described the differences between the United States and other countries (Chapter 2) and have explained those differences in terms of a prevailing American ideology (Chapter 3). But *why* do Americans hold to those ideas about the proper role of government? We now turn to answers to that question.

4

Why Do Americans
Think That Way?

I sn't it an interesting puzzle? Why do Americans think about the proper role of government differently than citizens of other countries do? The answer to that question turns out to be quite complicated. There are several theories abroad in the scholarly writing on the subject. In this chapter I present some of those theories, attempt to assess the plausibility of each, and tie them together into as coherent an explanation as I can. As I understand the existing literature, there is no single theory to which most writers on the subject subscribe. But I will try to synthesize various concepts into a theory of "path dependence" according to which early events in American history started the country down the path of limited government, subsequent events reinforced that direction, and the distinctive pattern lasted to the present.

As was evident in the last chapter, many scholars believe that political culture is not a very satisfying explanation for the differences among countries. One reason for their skepticism is that "culture" is often a kind of residual category, what a comparativist trots out to explain differences among countries when all else fails. As such, culture has a sort of elastic quality; it's a concept that can be stretched too far. If culture can be extended like that to explain everything, then it ends up explaining nothing.

That skepticism about culture as an explanation for differences among countries might be justified if the matter rested, in effect, with the statement, "Culture did it." But we can enhance the explanatory power of cultural or idea-based explanations if we are able to pinpoint the origins of the ideas. While the observation, "Americans are as they are because they are as they are" doesn't make for a very satisfactory theory, we can make more progress by exploring *why* Americans think as they do and value the things they value. Exploring those origins of American ideology is what this chapter is about.

This chapter falls into five major categories of explanation: migration, diversity and localism, economic and social structure, opportunity, and isolation from other countries. We'll proceed through each of them in turn and then tie them together. The theory of path dependence, which does the work of integrating these various explanations, will be presented in the conclusion of this chapter.

MIGRATION

Let us begin at the beginning, with the types of people who came to America and their descendants. The central proposition about migration is quite straightforward: American values are connected to the kinds of people who came here. But the key point is that many of the people who traveled to these shores were systematically and fundamentally different from those who stayed behind in the old countries. They therefore brought ideas about government and politics with them that were systematically different from the ideas of the people who remained. Those ideas in turn affected, and still affect, American institutions and public policies.

Why did people come to America? In simple terms, there are four categories of people in the American population, each composed of immigrants and their descendants. The four are as follows:

1. Some people moved to America to escape unacceptable religious or political status back in their homelands. Such status ranged from being deprived of privileges because of religious beliefs to suffering various penalties to actual persecution. Included in this category are early religious groups like the Pilgrims and Puritans. Lipset (1979:Ch.4) argues that the prevalence of these sorts of immigrants in the early days meant that America came to be dominated by Protestant sects (e.g. Methodists, Baptists) as opposed to adherents of established churches like the Church of England or the Roman Catholic Church. Members of those Protestant sects brought with them a distinctive moral code and a view of religious and political authority that was very different from the orientations of people in established churches who tended to stay behind in the old countries. These Protestants were distinctively suspicious of authority and hierarchy, given their experience, their faith, and their opposition to traditional religious and civil authority. We'll trace the results of those differences in a moment.

2. Some people migrated to America for economic reasons. But there were two kinds of economically motivated immigrants. The first kind were down and out in the old country and came to America to escape poverty or even threatened starvation. The second kind may not have been in desperate economic situations in the old country. But they perceived America to be the land of opportunity, particularly economic opportunity, and came to America to become better off than they were. In both cases, a few hardy souls immigrated first. They then sent back word to relatives and friends that there was land or other economic opportunity. Those people came to join them, sometimes in a rush of immigration and at other times in smaller numbers over a longer period of time. So there might be a small

rural community of Norwegians in Minnesota or Wisconsin, for instance, all of whom came from the same small part of Norway, sometimes from the same valley. They settled in close proximity, and several generations did the same before the community started to disperse.

3. The third category of immigrants came to America against their will. The most noticeable among this population were blacks, brought to America as slaves, and their descendants. The legacy of this kind of "immigration" has been profound throughout American history, and lasts to the present day. The founders compromised over counting slaves; the Civil War was fought partly over slavery; the civil rights movement of the 1950s and 1960s affected us fundamentally; and Americans still grapple with issues like affirmative action, racial prejudice, housing segregation, and employment discrimination.

4. Some people were here before the first Vikings visited these shores and before Columbus landed. American Indians crossed the Bering Strait centuries earlier. Their descendants made up many nations, some of them settled largely in one place and some of them nomadic, scattered across the whole of North America.

Over the course of American history, the first two categories came to dominate American politics. Indians were conquered, many of them brutally exterminated and many of the remainder herded into reservations. To the extent that Indians emphasized community values, the dominant culture and politics might have been more community-oriented and less individualistic if more of them had survived. But as history unfolded, they were in fact nearly eliminated.

Those who came to these shores against their will, of course, did not dominate the political landscape either. Blacks were kept in slavery until the Civil War, and have been kept subordinate since. In terms of both numbers and political power, they too were relegated to a distinct minority status. Issues of race, of course, have remained profoundly troubling and divisive to the present day. Despite the importance of these issues, however, and acknowledging the important contributions of blacks and Indians to American society, economics, and politics, it would still be hard to argue that they came to dominate the country.

The people who did come to dominate American society, economics, and politics were those in the first two categories, those who came to escape unacceptable religious or political status in their old countries and those who came for economic reasons. Let's discuss them in order.

The first category, those who came to escape religious or political conditions that they found unacceptable and wished to practice their religion as they saw fit free of interference, understandably brought with them a profound aversion to governmental and religious authority. Methodists in England, for instance, left for America because they found unacceptable and even abhorrent the power of the established Church of England, the taxes they were required to pay for its maintenance, and the close alliance between religious and governmental authority. Little wonder that such people would believe in obedience to established religious and political authority less than adherents of the Church of England who stayed behind. Those who moved to America were not the same as those who stayed. And their skepticism about authority, hierarchy, and obedience contributed to a distinctive American political culture that persisted through subsequent generations.

Note that I am not making an argument about Weber's "Protestant ethic." It's not necessary to argue that American Protestants were distinctively hardworking, and I don't want to hinge an argument about American distinctiveness on the importance of Protestantism. As Shklar (1991:71) points out, "Why, after all, have Chinese, Irish, and Jewish Americans worked as maniacally as they have? Not because they were Protestants." Shklar may be right, and there may still be an immigration selection process at work. That's because some of the non-Protestant people to whom she refers may have migrated to America for economic reasons, a point we discuss shortly. Regardless of ethnicity and religion, in other words, it's likely that people who came to America were atypically interested in pursuing the "American dream," where hard work rather than inheritance is supposed to gain you economic advancement, and thus were more acquisitive and individualistic than Europeans who stayed home (Lipset 1979:58). The argument about Protestant sects that I set forth above refers not to economic reasons for moving, which apply much more broadly than to Protestants alone, but to the distrust of authority that came from the feeling of oppression at the hands of the established religions of Europe. Lipset (1977:86), citing Tyler, sums up the situation in America thus: "The continent was peopled by runaways from authority."

Now there is some tension between the orientations of the early religious communities and the value placed on individualism which I described in the last chapter. Early Puritan communities, for instance, were hardly places where individual autonomy and freedom were prized. In some respects, in fact, one could say that they were quite tyrannical, insisting on the subordination of the individual to the mindset of the community. For the argument in this book, however, the key is localism (which I discuss in this chapter). Even in religious communities that were quite closed and tyrannical, there was still a fierce sense of independence from a larger set of religious or political authorities. Both routes—the individualism resulting from the value placed on economic advancement and the local autonomy of religious communities—led to the same place: an abiding distrust of government authority and a distinct preference for limited government.

The second category consists of those who came to America for economic reasons. It seems quite natural that many of them would value individual economic advancement and the acquisition of material goods and wealth. After all, that was their purpose. As Borjas (1990:3) puts it, immigrants shared "a common vision: the belief that the United States offered better opportunities for themselves and for their children than did their countries of origin." That value placed on economic advancement in turn played a part in creating the individualistic and antistatist culture described in the last chapter. The main goal in life for such people would understandably be their own economic well-being and that of their families and descendants.

This orientation also resulted in the distinctive American aversion to government, and particularly to taxation. If my purpose is to create my own wealth, then of course taxation is confiscating what is mine, and I have every interest in keeping taxes as low as possible. By extension, I have every interest in keeping the reach and expense of government as small as possible. So many people who came to America for economic reasons adopted these ideas, and they passed them on to their children and to future generations.

There were, of course, important differences among the economic reasons that prompted those who left their homes and traveled to these shores. Not all of them, even those who came for economic reasons, were entrepreneurial risk takers bent on the acquisition of wealth, the seizing of opportunity, and the promotion of their individual advancement. Irish escaping the potato famine, for instance, were simply desperate. Men other than firstborn sons in societies governed by primogeniture, having no way to make a living without the ability to inherit land, might have been more or less forced to move. Criminals and indentured servants might similarly have traveled to America without much entrepreneurial motivation. Not all reasons for traveling to America, in other words, even economic ones, would contribute to the distinctive individualistic and antigovernment political culture that we have discussed.

Still, it is likely that at least some of those who came to America for economic reasons were systematically different from those who stayed behind. That is, some of them—enough to make a difference—would have been more concerned with their individual economic advancement and would probably have been more unhappy about taxation than those who stayed behind in the old countries. Because of that tendency, the center of American politics was pushed in a more individualistic and antigovernment direction, on average, than the center of other countries. As Borjas (1990:3) summarizes the point, "Immigrants are not typical individuals. People willing to make a costly and uncertain investment in the American dream are quite different from the millions who choose not to migrate at all, or who choose to migrate elsewhere." Although the empirical evidence on this point about the difference between those who came to America and those who stayed behind would be harder to obtain this far after the fact than we might like, it seems likely that many immigrants were more entrepreneurial and more amenable risk-taking than those who stayed behind—it was risky to come here.

So it makes sense to argue that there were probably substantial differences between those who came to these shores and those who stayed behind. It certainly makes sense that those who traveled to America were not a random sample of the population in the country from which they came. After all, they did come for some reason.

DIFFERENCES AMONG IMMIGRANTS

We don't want to make the mistake of portraying immigrants as homogeneous. In fact, there were profound differences among immigrants. In particular, the early Protestant immigrants were quite different from the later waves of immigrants—Irish, Italian, Eastern European, many of them Roman Catholic. In his analysis of the first part of the twentieth century, Hofstadter (1963:8–9) describes the clash of cultures between Progressive reformers, largely agrarian or middle-class Protestant Yankees, and recent immigrants, who were very much adherents of the big-city political machines that the reformers were trying to destroy. Balogh (1991) has a somewhat different view of the interests allied with the Progressives, adding to agrarian interests the emerging urban middle class, which was also opposed to urban party machines. In any event, to the recent immigrants, Hofstadter (1963:183) says, "The reformer was a mystery. Often he stood for things that to the immigrant were altogether bizarre, like women's rights and Sunday laws, or downright insulting, like temperance." These later immigrants were more accustomed to religious or political hierarchy than the early Protestants, more likely to be industrial workers, and much more tied to big-city political machines. They were also major supporters of the policies of the New Deal in the 1930s, which expanded the reach and size of government considerably. If Hofstadter is right, the history of the United States in the first part of this century represented a titanic battle between agrarian, small-town, middle-class, individualistic Protestants from old Yankee stock and recently arrived urban, working-class, Catholic immigrants who espoused a quite different set of values.

It would be hard to maintain, of course, that all of American political culture is cut from the same cloth. In the last chapter, indeed, I specifically avoided claiming that such a homogeneous individualistic culture existed. But let's remind ourselves of several important considerations. First, many of the more recent immigrants, while not of traditional Protestant stock and values, still fell into the category of those who came to these shores seeking economic advancement. As such, at least some of them might well have been more likely to be entrepreneurial and risk-taking than those who stayed in the old countries. That observation holds true not just for many of the Irish, German, Italian, and Eastern European immigrants, but for recent Hispanic and Asian immigrants.

Second, we need to remind ourselves yet again that we're trying to compare the center of American politics and the center of the politics of other industrialized countries. Despite the differences among the various kinds of immigrants, it still could be that the central tendency of American immigrants was more antistatist and more distrustful of authority than those who stayed behind in their countries of origin. If that is true, then the presence of even some such immigrants would push American politics more to the right than the politics of their countries of origin.

Third, as we noticed in our discussion of the weakness of political parties in Chapter 2, the reforms that started in the Progressive era did eventually succeed in weakening the parties, state by state, locality by locality, throughout the twentieth century. Civil service reform severely eroded the power of patronage, and the direct primary broke the parties' lock on nominations. And as noted in Chapter 3, the tendency to criminalize some activities that are legal and tolerated in other countries might be related to the importance of some versions of Protestant morality.

CANADIAN-AMERICAN DIFFERENCES

One set of early Americans did not share the distrust of authority that we have been discussing: Loyalists to the British crown, many of them Anglicans, believed in obedience to authority and loyalty to British rule. The continued presence of these "Tories" in large numbers after the American Revolution would have complicated considerably the story of migration I have told here, because they did not subscribe to the individualism, localism, and distrust of governmental and religious authority that I have argued were the hallmarks of American political thought.

But as losers in the Revolution, they migrated to Canada or returned to Britain in large numbers, voluntarily or involuntarily, leaving very few of their adherents behind (Lipset 1990). Conversely, the more individualistic sympathizers with the American Revolution in Canada left there to come to the United States (Lipset 1996:91). Thus did migration once again enhance the distinctive American orientation toward government; those who did not share that orientation left, and those who did share it came.

Lipset (1990) uses that migration of Tories to Canada to explain many differences between the United States and Canada. Less concerned with limiting government, Canada elected to adopt a Westminster-type parliamentary system. Later, Canada adopted a larger welfare state than the one that emerged in the United States, including (fairly recently) national health insurance. Canadians, according to Lipset, have been less tolerant than Americans of violence and vigilantism, which are extensions of individualism; and Canada therefore enjoys crime rates lower than those in the United States. Lipset (1990:140–142) also presents data showing that both elites and the mass public in Canada, by a variety of measures, favor "big government" more than similar Americans.

Lipset's theory of migration resulting in a more "Tory touch" in Canada than in the United States has its critics. Perlin (1997), for example, comparing survey data in the two countries, concludes that Canadians are every bit as capitalistic, individualistic, and egalitarian as Americans are. But Perlin (1997:103) does find "one significant exception. Canadians, collectively, seem more willing than Americans to use government in an active role to pursue both economic and social objectives." That is indeed a significant exception, for it bears directly on both the institutional design and the shape of public policy in the two countries.

It seems likely that a similar interaction between ideology and institutions to which we pointed in the American case operated in Canada as well. But partly because of the migration to which Lipset refers, Canada's interaction worked differently. Canadians constructed stronger governmental institutions, including a parliamentary system. They provided for stronger political parties, some of which turned out to be innovative proponents of social programs like health insurance, first in selected provinces and then nationally. They designed public policies more ambitious than those of the United States, though less ambitious than those of many European countries. Thus the Westminster system and the relatively Tory values in Canada reinforced each other, resulting in a larger and stronger state than the American state, just as the American fragmented institutions and individualistic values reinforced each other. This may not explain all the differences between Canada and America, but there seems to be something to it.

In any event, the overarching point to remember is that migration is a selection process. People who move, on average, are systematically different from people who stay behind. Or to put it in statistical terms, people who move are a biased sample of the entire population from which they are selected. Norwegians who came to America were different from Norwegians as a whole, as the English who came were different from the English as a whole, and so forth. That's one reason America was different from other countries, even before the Constitution was written, and since.

DIVERSITY AND LOCALISM

I started Chapter 3 with a story about American diversity, my hypothetical answer to the question about what America is really like. It's true that this country presents a stunning array of differences: regional, racial, ethnic, class, and others. Combined with that diversity is a pervasive localism. Much more than people in most other industrialized countries, Americans are inclined to leave power in state and local hands.

That localism began, once again, at the beginning. America began as thirteen separate colonies. Actually, it began more locally than that—in local communities, many of them religiously based, in which the culture was so communitarian as to be tyrannical. One plausible model of the evolution of government in this situation, in fact, is that governments within each colony were constructed as rather weak governments, to allow these local communities their treasured autonomy. Then the logic of weak government within colonies was eventually transferred to the design of the national institutions.

At any rate, there were striking differences among the colonies. Some sanctioned slavery; others did not. Some were dominated by Protestant sects; others were not. They contained very different sorts of immigrants. And they had dissimilar economies. The one thing that tied them together at the time of the Revolution was their opposition to British rule.

Given the diversity among the colonies, it is hardly surprising that there was some difficulty in linking them once the American Revolution had been won. The Articles of Confederation was the first try. The Articles bound the thirteen former colonies into a loose confederation, in which each retained a good deal of autonomy. After only a few years of experience with the Articles, however, the disadvantages of that sort of confederation became apparent. The former colonies were even exacting tariffs on goods transported from one to another.

The result was the Constitution. But the trick during that long hot summer of 1787 in Philadelphia (see Jillson 1988) was to work out a way to achieve some greater centralization without at the same time cutting too far into the autonomy of the individual states. The federal system was the solution to this dilemma. Some powers would be given to the national government, which would be supreme in its sphere, but many powers would be reserved to the states. The founders also addressed the fundamental question of whether the new Constitution was a union of states or a union of people, answering, "Both." So they established a bicameral Congress; the Senate, composed of equal representation for each state; and the House of Representatives, apportioned by population. Thus were localism and states' rights enshrined in the Constitution, which has lasted to the present day.

The United States, of course, is not the only industrialized country that has adopted a federal system. Canadian provinces, for example, have a constitutional autonomy that is similar to the autonomy of American states. Some version of a federal system is a standard response the world over to the generic problem of forging a single country from highly diverse localities. The point is not to argue that America is unique in this respect, but only to emphasize that federalism in America powerfully reinforced the fragmentation of institutions that was implied in the separation of powers, checks and balances, and bicameralism. That fragmentation, the product of the American belief in limited government, resulted in the messy and unwieldy institutional setup that has become both our wonder and our exasperation.

American localism was fundamentally related to another practice that was distinctively American: slavery. Blacks were brought by force to these shores from Africa, treated as property, and enslaved on plantations in the South. To abolitionists, slavery was a moral outrage, and its practice played major parts in many signal events in our history. Slavery was a knotty problem in the very formation of the Union, as some people sought its abolition and southerners staunchly defended it as part of their way of social and economic life. The issue of how to count slaves for the purposes of the census and congressional apportionment plagued the 1787 constitutional convention, and was resolved only by the uneasy compromise of counting each slave as three-fifths of a person. Whether new states would be admitted to the Union as slave states or free states was a fundamental conflict as the country expanded. And the Civil War, the bloodiest war in American history, was fought partly over general issues of states' rights, partly over economic conflicts between the relatively urbanized North and the agrarian South, but also partly over slavery.

Slavery was intimately tied to localism. Southern arguments for states' rights were very much driven by Southern interest in resisting abolitionist sentiment in the North (Hartz 1955:147). If states' prerogatives could be preserved, then slavery could be preserved as well. Conversely, if the nation were to adopt a unitary constitutional system without federalism, slavery would be jeopardized. Thus was slavery a major driving force in the adoption and maintenance of a federal system of government.

The more general diversity and localism in the country, of course, argued for the design of a federal system in any event. But the system of slavery added a powerful southern impetus to preserve the prerogatives of states and localities to conduct their business as they saw fit, free of what they would have seen as national interference. And even after slavery was abolished, its legacy of opposition to the national government in the name of states' rights continued.

There have been changes over the years, of course, in the distribution of powers between the American national government and the states. One of the reasons the Constitution has endured for more than two hundred years, in fact, has been its flexibility to allow change in the face of changing conditions and problems. Only some of those changes have come about through constitutional amendment. Many more of them have involved court interpretation of constitutional language. The Constitution, for instance, gives the power to regulate interstate commerce to the national government. That power has been interpreted through the years very broadly, so that conditions affecting commerce, economic regulations of various kinds, even civil rights laws and certain police powers—combating kidnapping, gambling, and prostitution, for example—have all been found to be appropriate exercises of the power of Congress to regulate interstate commerce. Racial discrimination in public accommodations such as restaurants and hotels, for instance, has been banned by federal action, pursuant to the power of Congress to regulate conditions affecting interstate commerce.

Even with these changes, however, the Constitution reserved, and still reserves, considerable power to the states and localities. They have their own powers to tax and spend. They are responsible, in the main, for education, streets and highways, police functions, the conduct of elections, and many other important aspects of government. State courts interpret their own states' laws and constitutions, and interpret contracts within their states, independent of federal court supervision. Many national programs, including welfare, Medicaid, interstate highways, and others, are actually federal-state collaborations, in which the federal government gives grants to the states in return for state adherence to federal requirements. And the country is currently conducting a momentous debate about which functions should be sent back to the states and which should be retained by the federal government.

One result of this decentralization of public policy is that marked differences exist between one locality and another. In education, for instance, curricula and spending per pupil vary tremendously from one state to another, a situation that is baffling to, say, French educators accustomed to a national education system. Observers and visitors from other countries are similarly baffled by local differences in American speed limits, enforcement of traffic laws, drinking age, welfare eligibility, abortion availability, and many other policies that are often determined nationally in their countries. Finally, variations among states and localities in regulatory regimes (e.g. licensing, environmental and employment regulations, taxes, and procedures for filing suits) dramatically raise the transaction costs of conducting interstate commerce, since business firms must spend a lot of money on lawyers and accountants that they would not have to spend if standards were national.

To return to the major point, America is a highly diverse country, with many differences from one locality to another. One major way in which that diversity has been handled, keeping the country together while still preserving a degree of local autonomy, has been the institution of a federal system. Thus American state governments, in contrast to the regional governments of some other industrialized countries, have their own powers and their own sovereignty, within the framework of the federal system. Add to this constitutional feature of federalism the more general localism of the country. When we have a problem, we look not just to Washington for solutions but to state and local governments as well. We even think of ourselves, as not simply Americans but also New Yorkers, Californians, Michiganders, and so forth.

One result of this diversity and localism is that there is more resistance to national initiatives than in most other industrialized countries. It has become practically a cliche in the United States, for instance, to decry a "one size fits all" approach to economic or social problems as we debate public policy issues. Throughout our history, "states rights" has often been a catch phrase used to resist the initiatives of the federal government, even in such areas as abolition of slavery and civil rights. We tend, more than citizens of other countries, to think that public policies should be tailored to local conditions, particularly in such areas as education and police powers. Diversity means to us, more than it means to people in other countries, that national policies won't work well and that government "closer to the people" will work better. The truth of these perceptions, of course, is a matter of considerable dispute. But it does seem that American diversity and localism lead to this sort of thinking.

Part of this resistance to national initiatives in the United States involves the operation of political parties, which have traditionally been local organizations. The classic urban political machines like Tammany Hall in New York and the Daley machine in Chicago were built on a very local exchange: favors like city jobs and services from the machine in return for electoral and financial support. So not only have American political parties been weak compared to parties in other countries (a phenomenon described in Chapter 2), but they have also been local. Indeed, localism has contributed to the weakness of the national parties. Through much of the twentieth century, for example, it was extremely difficult for the national Democratic Party to discipline Southern Democrats in Congress. Southerners actually held the balance of power, in fact, partly because they benefited from the seniority system that allocated committee chairs, and partly because they could build majorities with Republicans without concern for party discipline. This decentralization of parties has added to the tradition of localism in the United States and has provided another reason for Americans, particularly those with partisan power, to resist the nationalization of politics.

All of this means that Americans want to limit, not just government in general but the national government in particular. Thus do diversity and localism contribute to the powerful interaction between ideas and institutions with which we began.

ECONOMIC AND SOCIAL STRUCTURE

The American economic and social structure also added its increment to the combination of ideas and institutions and the importance of diversity and localism. Many observers have noticed that American class conflict is muted relative to other countries. There are obvious differences, of course, between rich and poor, haves and have-nots, and the upper and lower classes. But compared to many industrialized countries, conflict among these economic and social strata seems to be less intense in the United States. Many Americans even go so far as to deny the importance of class differences, as part of their ideology of equality. The very concept of class makes Americans vaguely uncomfortable.

In his much-noted work on American distinctiveness, Hartz (1955) traces this muted class conflict, and its resulting ideology of limited government, to the lack of a feudal past in America. In the Middle Ages in most European countries, economies and societies had a feudal structure. Lords or nobility owned huge tracts of land, and passed their land on to their own heirs. Most people were vassals or serfs, farming and living on the land without owning it, in return for fees paid to the lords. One was born into one's station in life, and there was precious little opportunity for advancement. This feudal system was accompanied in most countries by a hereditary monarchy and by an established church that was part of the ruling class. Thus privilege and station were not only economic facts of life; they were also thought to be ordained by God.

According to Hartz, the demise of this feudal system in most of the countries of Europe set in motion a vigorous and often violent class conflict, as the serfs and their descendants clashed with the lords and their descendants. After all, the feudal system had established clear divisions in these societies along class lines, and it's little wonder that class differences should become class conflicts as feudalism decayed and eventually disappeared. Class thus became a standard, natural concept in the thinking of most Europeans, a completely understandable legacy of a feudal system. Even when feudal systems disappeared, people were still accustomed to the notion that they were born into a "station in life," that some folks were "naturally" richer than others, and that people were limited in their opportunities to move up social and economic ladders.

Hartz points out that America had no feudal system and therefore experienced no revolt of the serfs, no revolution based on class warfare, and comparatively little in the way of class conflict. As Hartz (1955:6) observes, "It is not accidental that an America which has uniquely lacked a feudal tradition has uniquely lacked also a socialist tradition. The hidden origin of socialist thought everywhere in the West is to be found in the feudal ethos." The result in the United States was less pressure from the left, less of a Marxist tradition due to less class consciousness, correspondingly less pressure for government action and government programs intended to redress economic imbalance, and more of a belief in the virtues of limited government. Hartz (1955:123) notes that in contrast to Europe, American farmers were as much landowners as they were peasants and laborers, both agrarians and capitalists; and American laborers could be labor, propertied, and individualistic all at the same time. Lipset (1977) adds, interestingly enough, that various Marxist theorists—Marx himself, Engels, Trotsky, Gramsci—had come to a similar conclusion, that America's nonfeudal past resulted in little working-class consciousness and the dominance of an ideology of individualism and antistatism.

Hartz goes on to discuss some rather subtle effects of this lack of a feudal past. One of them is that there was less need in America than in Europe to construct strong governmental institutions like parliamentary systems and strong political parties, because Americans did not need to worry about using such institutions to combat the remnants of a ruling class rooted in feudal privilege (Hartz 1955:44). Another is that the American

Revolution was quite different from, say, the French Revolution, in that Americans did not require a revolution that would establish their equality in a class structure or remake their society. Hartz (1955:96) notes that in America, there was "the absence of an aristocracy to fight, the absence of an aristocracy to ally with, and the absence of a mob to denounce." Shklar (1991) adds that earning a living is a tremendously important American value, which means that many Americans have equal contempt for idle aristocrats, slaves, women at home, and the unemployed.

Another effect of feudalism is that migration again played a role, since people came to these shores to escape feudal and postfeudal shackles and therefore did not bring with them the intellectual baggage that characterized those who stayed behind. This was, in Lipset's (1979) felicitous phrase, "The First New Nation," free of a feudal past and even free of the values and orientations that went with the aftermath of a feudal past. It was composed of people who, in Tocqueville's phrase, were "born equal," and did not need to fight for equality.

Hartz, of course, has had his critics. Some criticize cultural approaches in general, of which Hartz's is one, pointing to the importance of institutions rather than widely held values or cultural norms. Others doubt the story line about muted class conflict, emphasizing the differences between haves and have-nots and noting, as we did when discussing equality of result, that the gap between rich and poor is actually much greater in America than it is in other industrialized countries. Other critics doubt that, even if culture is important, Hartz has correctly identified the themes of that culture. Katznelson (1986:37), for instance, points out that most American industrial workers were not like the original Protestant individualists, but were ethnic Catholic immigrants. Thus Hartz's liberal tradition could not have been the result of "an easy intergenerational transfer of values," partly because these immigrants came from societies that did have a feudal tradition. Still other critics grant that Hartz describes a part of reality but dispute the notion that his liberal tradition was or is the consensus or dominant political culture, pointing instead to various strands of American political thought in addition to liberalism. Finally, Foner (1984) argues that the American South actually was a feudal system of a sort, which should have produced a high degree of class conflict if the aftermath of feudalism worked as Hartz describes it. But European-style class conflict did not emerge in the South, because race intervened to divide the working class. In fact, those in power in the South exploited race to accomplish exactly that division, by pitting poor whites against blacks.

I discussed some of these criticisms in the last chapter. With regard to the importance of institutions, for instance, I concluded that a powerful interaction between political culture and institutions is at work, rather than either of them being dominant. I also pointed out different themes in American political culture, including both individualism and communitarianism, but concluded that in the American context, they all tended to point to an emphasis on limited government and localism. I recognized earlier in this chapter the differences among immigrants but maintained that some of the later immigrants came to America for economic reasons, bringing with them the values of individual acquisition and equality of opportunity. I emphasized the importance of elections as a specific mechanism by which culture and public policy might be linked. I also reminded us of our main task here, to compare the American political center to the centers of other countries.

Specifically with regard to the connection between the lack of feudalism and American values, the South is indeed something of an anomaly. It seems to me that the southern experience really does not fit the Hartzian argument about the impact of the lack of a feudal past, partly because, as Foner suggests, race intervened.

But there also seems to me to be something to the argument about feudalism. As we're trying to construct a story of path dependence here, a major feature of American history is that the country was starting from scratch, so to speak, free of an economic and social system that had dominated the countries of Europe for centuries. That lack of a feudal legacy in this country, combined with the values of immigrants who were trying to escape that legacy in their old countries, was bound to affect American values.

There is another line of argument about the American class structure. We'll ask why in a moment, but just descriptively, labor unions in the United States are somewhat different from those in other countries. American unions concentrate on getting better pay and fringe benefits, more job stability, and better working conditions for their members. In the process, they are not as involved in pressuring for a more ambitious welfare state for all citizens as are unions in many other countries. American unions, of course, have not eschewed such involvement entirely. They were strong supporters of Medicare and the War on Poverty in the 1960s, for example, and have pushed for social programs for much of the post-World War II period. But in comparison, unions in other industrialized countries lead larger movements advocating, enacting, and protecting a much more sweeping welfare state than exists in the United States.

In those other countries, furthermore, unions are often intimately involved in democratic socialist political parties. The link between unions and those parties is much closer than the link between American unions and the Democratic Party. Again, we shouldn't portray American unions as utterly different. Greenstone (1969) documents the ways in which trade union officials organized election campaign work and recruited rank-and-file union members into campaign activity, and he also documents the emergence of organized labor as a major adjunct of the national Democratic Party. Still, with some exceptions such as Detroit, Greenstone does not find that unions are as fully integrated organizationally into the Democratic Party in this country as they are into democratic socialist parties in European countries.

There has never been the tradition of viable democratic socialist parties in America, furthermore, that one finds in most European countries. A substantial literature exists on why there's no socialism in the United States (e.g., Lipset 1977; Foner 1984). Fringe socialist parties have emerged, but none that had a real chance to attain power or even a share of power. The Democratic Party in the United States, for instance, has never been a socialist party in the tradition of the pre-1990s British Labour Party or the democratic socialist parties in most of continental Europe. That is, no viable American party has advocated state ownership and control of economic production, close state regulation of the economy, or a really thoroughgoing welfare state that is financed, owned, and operated by the government.

Lipset (1977:93–96) observes that American radicalism has also had a different character from European radicalism. The 1960s left wing in the United States, for instance, stressed decentralization and community control rather than centralism, which fits with American traditions of individualism and antistatism. Intriguingly, Lipset notices that both left and right in Europe have supported strongly centralized government, whereas both left and right in America have opposed centralization.

The weakness of pressure from the left is one of the main reasons that the United States has less ambitious domestic programs and a smaller public sector than is found in other industrialized countries. When Cameron (1978) compares countries and analyzes many variables that could account for their differences, he finds that one of the main reasons that some countries have a large public sector is that they have had viable, and even dominant, leftist parties for some of their history. And Heclo (1986) maintains that the poor are less well treated in American public policies than in other countries partly because their natural advocates, like activist labor unions and social democratic parties, are simply absent in the United States. The poor themselves are extremely hard to organize the world over, but the difference is that they have much better-organized advocates in other countries than they have in the United States.

Why has America, particularly the American labor movement and the political left, evolved as it has? A number of answers have been suggested in the literature. First, the suffrage came to American workers long before the Industrial Revolution did (Bridges 1986; Foner 1984; Lipset 1977). Particularly after property qualifications for voting were eliminated, there was universal white manhood suffrage very early in American history. This sequence of events meant that workers did not need to organize in both the political and economic spheres at once. In European countries, by contrast, workers were pressing for both the right to vote and the right to organize in the workplace at the same time, causing both unions and parties of the left to combine political and economic issues into one package, wrapped in a general rhetoric of class consciousness. But since American workers already had the suffrage and didn't have to organize to get it, American unions were able to devote themselves more single-mindedly to workplace issues.

This feature of American historical sequence thus accounts for the less political character of American labor unions relative to their European counterparts. Of course there is heavy union involvement in American politics. But compared to European unions, which have been intimately tied to social democratic parties and very much bound up with the concept of class struggle both politically and economically, American labor union activity has been more narrowly confined to workplace issues. As Shefter (1986:198) puts it, "American trade unionists at the end of the nineteenth century were not revolutionaries; they called strikes to extract concessions from employers, not to topple the state."

Second, going along with universal suffrage, political parties emerged in the United States before public bureaucracies did (Skowronek, 1982). Most European countries started with preexisting strong public bureaucracies, carryovers from such strong premodern institutions as monarchies or standing armies (Weir, Orloff, and Skocpol 1988:16). According to Shefter (1994), therefore, patronage wasn't available to European political parties, since people obtained and held jobs in autonomous public bureaucracies by some sort of merit criteria rather than by the intervention of party officials. This meant that the appeal of parties of the left was based on ideology, rather than patronage.

In the early United States, by contrast, strong government bureaucracies—federal, state, or local—did not emerge (Skowronek, 1982). Political parties emerged first, to organize the white men entitled to vote by widespread suffrage. Thus, Shefter argues, patronage was available to American parties, and particularly in the big cities, parties used patronage to claim and hold power, eschewing ideology. Thus parties of the left in the United States were less ideological, less radical, and less inclined to democratic socialism than leftist parties in Europe. But the corruption of the patronage base also fueled the reform movements that weakened American parties.

Orloff and Skocpol (1984) argue that the early twentieth-century British pattern of a strong civil service and programmatic parties made Britain a pioneer in welfare programs like workers' compensation, old age pensions, health insurance, and unemployment insurance. The American Progressive movement at about the same time failed to institute similar programs in such areas as pensions and social insurance. According to Orloff and Skocpal, Britain and America were roughly comparable at the time in industrialization, liberal values, and the demands of organized industrial workers. They attribute the differences in public policy instead to institutional or state-centered factors, particularly the combination of bureaucratic and party characteristics. America's relatively weak civil bureaucracy meant it had a lesser capacity than Britain to administer a welfare state, and the American patronage parties did not include the programmatic advocacy of the welfare state that British parties typified.

The third reason for the distinctive character of the working class and the absence of socialism in America is that the working class in the United

States has always been more racially and ethnically heterogeneous than in most European countries (Bridges 1986; Foner 1984; Lipset 1977). This heterogeneity means that a lot of workers' loyalty is ethnic or racial, rather than based on an explicit class consciousness. Indeed, racial tension within the working class has resulted in less pressure for government social programs, as white workers have opposed more vigorous approaches in programs like job training, affirmative action, and housing because they view such programs as benefiting blacks (Quadagno 1994:192). This kind of muting of class consciousness because of racial and ethnic heterogeneity is another reason that democratic socialism, based as it is on concepts of working-class solidarity, has less appeal in America than in Europe. The working class is simply less "solid."

Finally, Hattam (1992) points to the unusual power of the American courts. Comparing Britain and the United States, she notices that both started labor movements and both passed similar labor legislation to encourage and reinforce those movements. But relatively weak British courts did not challenge the legislation, whereas relatively strong and autonomous American courts did, either striking down the laws or interpreting them in such a way as to weaken them in application. Thus the American labor movement isn't nearly the political force that the British labor movement is, because American courts have stood in its way.

Thus there are several theories—the lack of feudalism, early universal suffrage and political party development, working-class heterogeneity, and the strength of the courts—that attempt to explain why class conflict is muted in the United States compared to other countries, why there is less working-class solidarity, why labor unions are less involved in partisan and electoral activity, and why there is no viable American democratic socialism. Regardless of which explanation or combination of explanations you might find most convincing, the consequence of the unusual American pattern is clear: much less pressure from the left for big government in the United States than in other industrialized countries. Thus these features of the American economic and social structure—the lack of a feudal past, the relatively narrow reach of labor unions, and the lack of viable democratic socialist movements—all contribute to our explanation of American distinctiveness. They help explain the unusual American belief in limited government and reinforce the combination of ideas and institutions with which the country started.

OPPORTUNITY

It's part of our national mythology that America is the land of opportunity. In some respects and for some of the people, the myth is true. To the extent that it is true, the pattern of opportunities in America has contributed to American distinctiveness.

The first point about opportunity flows from the point about the muted importance of class. In many European countries, power and privilege were the inherited province of the nobility and wealthy. One couldn't get ahead economically or socially without being born into privilege. One couldn't attend the best preparatory schools or universities, for instance, or aspire to the higher-status or wealthy professions, without being born into privilege. This lack of class mobility traditionally meant that opportunity for advancement was quite limited for much of the population.

America, by contrast, has allowed for greater occupational and social mobility. It's decidedly not true that every American is born on the same footing, of course. A considerable body of writing on life chances of various segments of the population shows that some people—because of race, gender, class, or other factors—simply don't have the same opportunities as others. But again, this is a book about America in comparative perspective. The issue is not whether America is the land of opportunity in some absolute sense, but rather whether America is the land of opportunity relative to other industrialized countries.

It would be hard to give iron clad proof either way. But this relative lack of hardened social classes and the sense that at least some are allowed to break out of their class of birth and move up in the world do lend some plausibility to the argument that greater opportunities for economic and social upward mobility have existed in the United States than in other countries. Without any history of royalty, nobility, feudal landholdings, or other such trappings of privilege, probably more people have actually had a good chance to move up, at least across generations and even within generations. And despite the presence of barriers to upward mobility in America, those barriers are probably less formidable than in other countries. I noted in my discussion of equality of opportunity in Chapter 3, however, that the difference in occupational and social mobility between the United States and other countries seems to be smaller lately than it used to be. Still, the impressive mobility early in American history, and the current perception of equality of opportunity, make America distinctive.

What does this greater opportunity have to do with American politics and public policy? The connection may seem a bit tenuous, but the notion is that opportunity enables individualism to flourish. If you believe that you can get ahead on your own, you feel less need to turn to government for help. Indeed, you might even feel that government could get in your way, either by taxing you at higher rates than you deem necessary or by regulating your business, career, or life in ways that retard your progress.

This logic turns only in part on the *reality* of opportunity. The *myth* of opportunity also promotes this train of thought. Even if people don't have equal access to opportunity, if they *believe* they have opportunities, they tend to adopt this individualistic, skeptical stance toward government. That's one reason that playing on class conflict in election campaigns, particularly by bashing the rich, doesn't work as well as one might think. Even people who aren't rich figure that they might one day become rich, or at least that their children might. So perceptions are at least as powerful as realities.

Another feature of the opportunity structure in America is Frederick Jackson Turner's (1920) theory of the frontier (see Taylor 1972). Turner believed that American culture and politics were profoundly shaped by the fact that the frontier was always available. If you weren't making it economically on the East Coast, or if you were politically oppressed, you could always cross the Appalachians and start a new life. Or if that didn't work, you could go to the Great Plains. The point is that the availability of the frontier created opportunities for people that they wouldn't have found in other countries. Turner thus called the frontier "this gate of escape," adding, "Men would not accept inferior wages and a permanent position of social subordination when this promised land of freedom and equality was theirs for the taking. . . . Free land meant free opportunities." (Taylor 1972:41)

The frontier then worked in the same way as other opportunities for individual advancement. People didn't need to turn to government for help or for basic services; if they weren't doing well in the East, they could just move west instead. To put it in a more general way, if the pie is always expanding, then government doesn't need to step in as much to redress grievances or set things right. If the private market provides, the thinking goes, government action is less necessary.

Wood (1992) also points out that widespread freeholding promoted equality. If farmers owned their own land in America, in contrast to the usual feudal European situation of peasants working for landholders, then it wasn't too great a stretch to conclude that they should be the equals of aristocrats. Turner also argued that, in view of widespread ownership of property on the frontier, a property-owning qualification for voting that existed in the East made a lot less sense. So a property qualification was abandoned in favor of universal manhood suffrage (for whites). According to Turner, the primitive conditions of the frontier, combined with the opportunity to own land, had a profoundly leveling effect; everybody was in the same boat.

Turner's thesis set off a huge historical literature, some of it critical and some of it written in support. Critics wrote that Turner neglected the pathologies of industrialism; understated the importance of slavery; ignored the fact that frontier institutions were borrowed from the East rather than the other way around; and overstated the tendency of the frontier to nationalize the country, homogenize the population, and promote equality. Supporters argued that while some of those criticisms might have merit, the central importance of the frontier in American historical development remained its impact on the sense of opportunity and hence on cultural and ideological structures that reinforced the American themes of individualism and skepticism about government.

Indeed, the availability of land promoted an entire intellectual tradition based on the virtue of ownership. Zundel (1995) discusses what he calls an agrarian republican ethical tradition. The notion is that owning a farm or other land creates civic virtue—it promotes values like responsibility, civic engagement, and family stability. Zundel argues that this tradition, developed originally in an agrarian setting, has created a set of symbols and values that have been transported even to rather unlikely contemporary settings. He shows that the agrarian republican language is used in modern debates about urban housing policy, for instance, as people extol the virtues of home ownership and the responsibility and stability that it supposedly brings to a community. And the American rate of private property ownership, especially home ownership, is in fact very high, compared to the rate in other countries.

In any event, the myth of America as a land of opportunity reinforced American individualism, the sense that people could take care of themselves and that government not only wasn't needed but might even get in the way. To the extent that the myth was punctuated by evidence of real opportunity, as with the availability of land on the frontier or evidence of actual occupational mobility, the impact of the structure of opportunities on American poltical thought was only made stronger.

ISOLATION

Finally, some additional factors, though not in and of themselves driving American distinctiveness, enabled America to be unlike other advanced industrialized countries. I will discuss two such enabling factors, international isolation and effects of war.

The United States has remained extraordinarily separate from other countries through much of its history. Part of that isolation is geographical. We're separated from other countries (except for Canada and Mexico) by vast oceans. European countries, by contrast, are thrown together much more. Even Great Britain, separated as it is from continental Europe by the English Channel, still is more closely tied to Europe than we are. Through all of the wars that pitted one country against another in Europe from the Middle Ages to nearly the present day, it was an inescapable fact that the fate of one country was intimately bound up with that of its neighbors.

American geographical isolation was accompanied by an economic isolation. Cameron (1978) shows that countries that are highly dependent on others for trade and capital grow larger public sectors than countries that are more isolated economically. Less independent countries can't manage their economies on their own and are obliged to cushion their citizens against the effects of international economic forces with social programs and countercyclical policies. Until recently, Cameron's argument goes, the United States depended much less than other industrialized countries on trade, capital flows across borders, and other economic exchange. This relative lack of interdependence enabled America to go its own way, with no need to bring its governmental policies or economic system into alignment with those of other countries, or to provide its citizens with cushions against international economic forces. The distinctive policies and practices I have described, though not necessarily caused by isolation, were able to continue without outside interference.

The most striking example of interdependence, of course, is the post–World War II development of the European Common Market, now the European Union. Started as a free trade zone, it developed into quite an elaborate set of common institutions, altering national sovereignty in important ways. Movement toward a common monetary system, for instance, has necessitated common policies concerning government deficits and social welfare spending. Indeed, the turmoil in France in 1996, in which government workers went out on strike and filled the streets in protest, was prompted by the European Union's insistence that France control its deficit by cutting government spending. The same set of issues resulted in the victory of the French leftist parties in the election of 1997. German efforts to trim governmental programs led 300,000 protesters to take to the streets in June of 1996.

The luxury of American isolation is changing as these lines are being written. Modern communications technology, for one thing, makes the world much more closely knit than it used to be. Rapid and reasonably priced airplane travel, television bounced off satellites, low-cost international telephone calls and faxes, and instantaneous electronic mail and computer hookups all enable the kinds of commercial and other transactions that we couldn't have dreamed of even three or four decades ago.

It is already apparent that the result of these developments is the decreasing isolation of the United States. More of America's economic activity is accounted for by international trade than it used to be. American industries are subjected to international competition that they weren't obliged to endure in earlier days. The economies of industrialized countries are more closely linked, and America is increasingly drawn into this global system. To add to the strictly economic factors, environmental protection is also reducing American isolation. Such environmental problems as ozone depletion, greenhouse gases, and reduction of the oceans' fishing stocks obviously don't respect geographical borders and require international cooperation to solve.

It seems unlikely, therefore, that the former geographic and economic isolation of the United States will continue to enable us to maintain as much of our distinctiveness as has been our custom. It's not clear in what respects and to what extent other countries will become like us, or we like them. All countries, furthermore, tend to find ways to maintain their own traditions. But it is possible that greater interdependence may foster, or even force, greater similarity among countries.

Finally, the effects of war, particularly the devastation of World War II, enabled the United States to go its own way. The War disrupted American economic and political routines, to be sure. But that disruption was much less severe than the disruption in Europe and Japan, where large portions of the transportation and communications infrastructure, industry, and housing stock were utterly destroyed. Little wonder that those countries turned to government to rebuild. American Marshall Plan aid, furthermore, which was designed to help rebuild Europe after World War II, went to public entities, not to private investment, adding another reason for government programs in Europe. Americans, on the other hand, were able to continue to resist massive government programs in such areas as transportation and housing after World War II because the country did not suffer wartime devastation.

CONCLUSION: A STORY OF PATH DEPENDENCE

Two roads diverged in a wood, and I —
I took the one less traveled by,
And that has made all the difference.

—*Robert Frost*

This chapter has tried to answer the questions, "Why do Americans at the center of our politics think the way they do about the proper role of government, and why have American government and public policy turned out to be as limited as they are, compared to other industrialized countries?" We have discussed several explanations, including migration, localism, economic and social structure, opportunity, and isolation. Let's try now to draw these explanations into an argument about why the United States is different.

That argument is a theory of path dependence (see Arthur 1988, 1994). Economic theories of path dependence were originally generated to explain why given technologies like the QWERTY typewriter keyboard (David 1985) or VHS video technology (Arthur 1988) came to dominate their markets, even though they may not have been the most efficient or advanced systems available. Once typewriters were designed with a QWERTY keyboard, for instance, everybody made an investment in that technology and then carried it over to computers. It's extremely difficult to replace QWERTY, even though better keyboards are possible (David 1985). For the same reason, VHS technology took over the video cassette market from Betamax technology once people made their investments in VHS, even though Beta may have been a better technology (Arthur 1988).

The central notion in path dependence is that a given system (e.g., a market or a country's governmental institutions) starts down a path and, once started, cannot easily reverse course. The notion is that initial conditions and early choices heavily affect the future course of events. The beginning choice may even be strictly random, as with the flip of a coin, or at least somewhat haphazard, though it may not be. Random or not, once initial choices are made, all of the involved agents invest in those choices, powerfully reinforcing the direction in which the system is headed. A slight edge in VHS market share over Betamax, for instance, powerfully affected which technology eventually took over. Arthur (1988, 1994) even argues that the system becomes "locked in" to its pattern. It might be possible to reverse direction, but very costly. Pierson (1996) makes a persuasive case that path dependence characterizes the political world even more often and more powerfully than it applies to economics.

Let us bring this theory to bear on differences between the United States and other industrialized countries. America started down the path of limited government very early. We started with a distinctive distrust of authority, including governmental authority, that sprang both from the values of the immigrants and from the pervasive localism of America. Faithful to and believing in that orientation, the founders deliberately built the country's fragmented governmental institutions (separation of powers, checks and balances, bicameralism, federalism) so as to limit government. Their design also contained specified limits on government action, as in the Bill of Rights, to be enforced by independent courts. Now that we have gone down that path of limited government for two centuries, we are extremely unlikely to design a wholly different set of institutions from scratch (North 1990:95). Some Americans think that the genius of the founders is their lasting legacy to all of us; others think that we're all stuck with these unwieldy institutions. Either way, there's no turning back.

A key starting point in an explanation for American peculiarity is the combination of ideology and institutions discussed at the end of Chapter 3. The American ideological center of gravity, which was more suspicious of governmental authority than the center of gravity in other countries, was systematically and deliberately built into our unusual institutions. So the idea of limited government became a hallmark, not only of some sort of general American political culture but also of the very structure of governmental institutions under which Americans still live. Those institutions consequently make change difficult and reinforce the ideology of limited government. This enduring and powerful interaction between ideas and institutions, each one reinforcing the other down through history, goes some way to explain the modern distinctiveness of American politics and public policy.

Let us explore the matter of institutional development a little more fully. North (1990) adapts the general principles of path dependence to understand institutional development. As North (1990:7) says, institutions "determine the opportunities in a society. Organizations are created to take advantage of those opportunities, and, as the organizations evolve, they alter the institutions. . . . [The result is] the lock-in that comes from the symbiotic relationship between institutions and the organizations that have evolved as a consequence of the incentive structure provided by those institutions."

To follow North's logic in the case of American governmental institutions, once the United States adopted a fragmented constitutional system, interest groups from the beginning right down to the present were formed and built their strategies around the institutions, creating powerful interactions between institutions and politics. Along the way, political parties—institutions that in other countries mobilize majorities, aggregate preferences, and organize government for action—were also severely weakened. As discussed in this chapter, the weakness of the administrative state through the nineteenth century was also a major part of the relative weakness of governmental institutions.

While some stories of path dependence start with a flip of the coin, I do not consider the initial steps in this case to have been a random start. To the contrary, the people who came to America and dominated our politics were, as noted earlier, systematically different from the people who stayed behind in their countries of origin. Because they came to these shores either to escape religious or political authority or to better themselves economically, the people who came to dominate American politics were more suspicious of government than those who populated other countries, more concerned about government tyranny, less given to obey authorities, less tolerant of hierarchy, more inclined to see taxation as confiscating what was theirs instead of as a way to finance collective purposes, and less inclined to support ambitious government programs.

In addition to a general suspicion of governmental authority to which migration patterns contributed, American diversity and localism resulted in a particular suspicion of the national government. Slavery reinforced localism powerfully, because it was the driving force for many arguments in favor of states' rights. Politics was local in many other respects, including the localism of our political parties. The constitutional establishment of a federal system ensured an institutional reinforcement of localism, as state and local governments retained a portion of their own sovereignty and powers.

Once the institutions were established and survived, the American ideology of limited government, the tradition of localism, and the workings of the institutions perpetually reinforced one another. Ideology dictated continued limits on government; but because government institutions were limited, people also developed limited expectations about what government could or should accomplish, reinforcing the ideas. As a theory of path dependence would have it, once America started down the path of limited government, it proved extremely difficult to change course, even if people were disposed to do so.

Arthur (1988) also argues that a direction in a path-dependent system can only be changed by some powerful coordination effect, such as an authoritative agency dictating a change by fiat. Such coordination is exactly what American institutions (fragmented governmental institutions and weak political parties) were designed to avoid, making a reversal of the initial course even less likely than with other cases of development.

In addition, interest groups have been built around these fragmented institutions. So when some proposal surfaces that would challenge the existing interest groups, these groups can block such a proposal more easily than with the more centralized or coordinated institutions in other countries. To block a proposal, a given interest group or coalition need only block it at one of several points (House committee, Senate floor, president, etc). To pass the proposal, it must survive all those challenges.

Margaret Thatcher could go farther and quicker in trimming the British welfare state than Ronald Reagan could go in this country, for example, because her parliamentary system gave her the coordination tools that the American system lacks (Pierson 1994). Not obliged to contend with the separation of powers, she could also count on the support of a strong, disciplined party in the British parliament. Even at that, according to Pierson, direct attacks on social programs in both countries were less effective than indirect strategies like institutional changes that strengthened budget cutters' hands or policies that weakened government revenue bases.

A similar logic applies to the notion of policy sequence (Weir 1992b). The idea is that public policies adopted early profoundly affect subsequent policies. The sequence starts with institutions that shape the alliances that are possible, guiding the development of ideas and the definition of people's interests. Government then adopts some public policy, like the New Deal version of employment policy in the 1930s. Those policies, once adopted, result in a set of beneficiaries or constituencies, who then organize interest groups to protect the policy in place (Walker 1991). Once a policy orientation is established, it becomes difficult to change course.

To return to our story, several other factors reinforced the original path. America's economic and social structure, first, shaped as it was by the lack of a feudal past, muted class conflict and discouraged the emergence of the democratic socialist tradition that one finds in most industrialized countries. As labor unions evolved in this country, they were more exclusively occupied with workplace issues than were labor unions in other countries, partly because they did not have to fight for the vote at the same time that they fought for benefits in the workplace. Neither the democratic socialist tradition nor the socialist parties that developed in many other industrialized countries ever emerged in the United States, for the variety of reasons we considered above. This lack of a democratic socialist movement and the somewhat narrower reach of American labor unions contributed substantially to this country's tradition of limited government, because there was less pressure from the left than is found in most other industrialized countries.

The myth and reality of opportunity, second, including the availability of the frontier, made it possible for people to advance on their own with less governmental protection than one observes in other countries. The third reinforcing factor, American geographic and economic isolation, though not driving the differences between the United States and other industrialized countries, further enabled us to go down a different path.

To summarize our theory of path dependence, migration and localism generated distinctive early American ideas, which centered on suspicion of authority and limitations on government. Those ideas were systematically built into American institutions, setting up the central interaction between those ideas and institutions that has affected our politics and public policies ever since. Once the limited government institutions were established, an entire structure of powerful interest groups and weak political parties reinforced the limitations that were hallmarks of both the ideas and the institutions. A number of other factors reinforced the American pattern of limited government: economic and social structure, including muted class conflict, the distinctive orientation of our labor unions, and the absence of democratic socialism and feudalism; the pattern of economic, social, and geographical opportunities; and relative isolation.

But in a system of path dependence, there is nothing historically inevitable or foreordained about such developments. Quite the contrary: Each choice on the path could go either way, there are no single or unique equilibria, and outcomes are not really predictable (Arthur 1988, 1994). The sequence is critical, but the outcome cannot be foreseen. If American labor unions had been fighting for the right to vote and for workplace rights at the same time a century after the adoption of the Constitution, for instance, political evolution in this country might have gone much more in the direction of "big government." Or if the United States had suffered as much destruction in World War II as European countries did, Americans might easily have resorted to much larger and more intrusive government to rebuild, instead of dismantling the massive government planning and rationing apparatus that was put in place during the wartime mobilization. This theory of path dependence, then, is quite different from historical determinism, and quite different from the determinism of various social science theories (Pierson 1996).

Indeed, the unfolding of American history is filled with critical junctures when there was conflict over institutional design and policy directions, when making a different choice would have gone against and then changed the prevailing ideas about limited government, and when in fact America did sometimes adopt measures that seemed much more like "big government" than the prevailing American ideology would have suggested. A vigorous debate was played out during the pre-Constitution period of the Articles of Confederation, for instance, about how much power the national government should have. The nation's history has been punctuated by similar debates ever since—between Federalists and Jeffersonians, Whigs and Jacksonians, nineteenth-century Republicans and Democrats, Progressives and their opponents, 1930s New Dealers and their opponents, and in our own day conservative Republicans and liberal Democrats. Some of those debates were about the proper role of the federal government vis-à-vis state and local governments; others were about government in general vis-à-vis the private sector.

No hegemonic Hartzian liberal consensus dominated those debates. Major choices were hotly contested at each juncture, and different choices would have altered the path that the country took. Those critical junctures were open policy windows (Kingdon 1995:Ch.8), opportunities for advocates of the expansion of the reach and size of government to make their case. And in fact, some "big government" initiatives were enacted. The New Deal programs of the 1930s, for instance, included social security, regulation of wages and hours, government employment programs, agricultural assistance, and securities and banking regulation. The federal government also introduced the expansive programs of the 1960s, including Medicare and Medicaid, civil rights legislation, federal aid to education, and the War on Poverty.

Those debates and governmental choices, however, took place in a distinctively American context. To return to a major theme of this book, those debates *centered* on a position concerning the appropriate powers and limits of government that was more to the limited government end of the continuum than the center in other countries. Although the outcomes of the struggles were not predetermined or inevitable, and although there were exceptions, the major choices in institutional design and public policy tended to point to a less expansive and more limited role for government than did similar choices in other countries.

This book has concentrated on critical turning points in American history that have led the country down our own path and so generated its distinctiveness. A similar analysis could be developed for other countries as well. For European countries, for example, the utter devastation of World War II would be one of those junctures, leading them to adopt more ambitious, government-centered programs to rebuild housing, transportation, and industrial infrastructure than they might have adopted without that devastation. Much earlier, it was the availability of a strong administrative state that enabled Bismarck to begin the development of far-reaching social welfare programs. A theory of path dependence, in other words, seems quite generally applicable, and probably helps us understand developments in all countries, not just the United States.

Some of the factors that led to American distinctiveness may be changing, although it's difficult to be confident about how much change is likely. New problems may also arise that call for new solutions. Globalization, for instance, could be making distinctiveness somewhat less possible and may increase the similarities among countries as the years go along. On the other hand, the logic of path dependence suggests that countries will not completely converge. So we turn last to some implications of American ideas and practices.

5

Implications

L et's first review where we have been. Chapter 2 described several fundamental differences between the United States and other advanced industrialized countries: institutions of government limited by the separation of powers and other deliberate aspects of constitutional design, relatively weak political parties, a smaller public sector compared to the size of the economy, lower taxes, and the narrower reach of our public policies. Chapter 3 attributed these differences between the United States and other countries to a prevailing American ideology at the center of our politics, which emphasizes the importance of limiting government; is suspicious of governmental and other authority; and seeks a smaller public sector, less ambitious public policies, and lower taxes than we observe in other countries. That ideology not only directly affects the formation of public policies but was also built into the structure of our institutions. Thus a powerful interaction between ideology and institutions, each reinforcing the other, started America down the path of limited government and contributed powerfully to American distinctiveness right down to the present day.

Chapter 4 presented some theories explaining why Americans think that way about the appropriate role of government and the limits that should be placed on governmental action. I attributed these distinctive American ideas first of all to the values and cultures of immigrants. Second, I argued, the diversity and localism of the country played into the ideology of limited government. Then other factors reinforced the interaction of ideas and institutions—the economic and social structure and muted class conflict, the myth and reality of opportunity, and America's isolation from other countries throughout most of its history. Chapter 4 ended with a "path dependence" account that tied these various factors together, emphasizing the early events that started America down the path of limited government, events that were then reinforced by subsequent developments. This theory of path dependence is the central concept that explains why America has come to be so different from other industrialized countries.

It's now time to ask what it all means. What can we learn from our differences with other industrialized countries? What are some pluses and minuses of the American way of approaching government? Should we consider thinking differently from the way we currently think? What is the future likely to hold?

LEARNING

Some might argue that America is unique and therefore can't learn much from other countries. The entire political culture—the intertwined system of values, norms, and practices—is so firmly established and so different from other countries that the practices of other countries could not be successfully transported to America. Beyond that, the governmental institutions are so stable and so important that what might work in a different institutional context won't work here. Even if people wanted to apply the experience of other countries to solve American problems, it would be argued, this powerful and unique combination of culture and institutions is bound to prevent the successful importation of others' policies and practices.

There's little doubt that America is different. But I still think we can learn from other countries. After all, the problems that we confront are not entirely different from those facing other countries. Although their solutions might have to be adapted, even in major ways, to fit the American cultural and institutional context, if they are successful in some way, their experience might point to some sensible solutions for us.

The case of health care illustrates the point nicely. As we have seen, in every other advanced industrialized country, virtually the entire population is covered by health insurance (White 1995a). Yet both the total per capita bill for medical care—public and private expenditures added together—and the total of medical care expenditure as a proportion of GDP are lower in those countries than in the United States. Morone (1990:268) points out that Canada, for instance, starting with a situation similar to the United States, adopted a national health insurance system that within a decade covered the entire population and actually reduced the share of Gross National Product (GNP) devoted to health care.

How can that be? How do these other countries achieve universal coverage at a lower cost? The answer is complicated, of course. American research and development, for instance, is unparalleled and expensive, incurring bills for the innovation of techniques and treatments that other countries never have to bear. Americans also prize convenience, and those who can afford it pay a high cost to avoid queues for treatment or delays in elective surgery.

But I believe that an important part of the answer lies in the themes of this book. Other countries achieve universal coverage at lower cost because of a degree of compulsion that Americans find difficult to tolerate. They require all employers to furnish health insurance to all employees, for instance; or they enroll all citizens in a government-sponsored insurance system and pay for it with higher taxes. They achieve cost control by such devices as setting global budgets and requiring providers to live within those budgets, negotiating fee schedules that will apply to all providers, rationing care, and other such practices. Patients may not be able to schedule elective procedures at their convenience but may have to wait in a queue. In other words, other countries compel people to do things they wouldn't otherwise do.

America started earlier in this century down the path of private health insurance, generally arranged as a fringe benefit at places of employment, instead of government health programs. Even if a universal government system at this stage would cost less in total taxes than the current mix of private insurance premiums, out-of-pocket payments, and government programs like Medicare and Medicaid, the nation has become so committed to private insurance, and so many interests (e.g., insurance companies and health care providers) have a stake in that system, that it would be very difficult to change direction now.

Perhaps, if compulsion were viewed differently in this country, people would be open to possible alternatives that they don't at present choose to take seriously. After all, elements of compulsion are already present in the American health care system; they just aren't government compulsion. Care is already rationed, for instance; it's just done by what somebody called the "wallet biopsy" rather than by some criteria other than wealth. Other rationing criteria might include determining who is sickest, what care is elective and what care is necessary, what care must be provided fast and what care can wait, who will benefit from the care the most, the importance of convenience, and so forth.

For another instance of compulsion in American health care, employers have taken lately to pushing employees into managed care rather than traditional fee-for-service care. The managed care companies in turn are quite strict about limiting access to specialists, shortening hospital stays, and implementing other cost-cutting measures. There's obviously an element of compulsion in that trend; it's just not government compulsion. And a political backlash is developing; new legislation has mandated forty-eight-hour hospital stays for mothers following normal deliveries, required that certain procedures be done in specified ways, and is starting to regulate managed care and the practice of medicine in other ways.

A different view of the appropriate role of government might allow for the possibility, for instance, of equating private health insurance premiums with taxes. They both come out of the same pocket, after all, so the issue isn't that taxes involve the greater compulsion; instead, the issue is what the money is buying. Or the type of national health insurance that works through employer mandates might be seen not as imposing an intrusive and burdensome requirement on small business but rather as a way of organizing to cover the whole population. But when it comes to taxes, we

Americans are so fundamentally antistatist that it makes a terrific difference to us whether we're paying for health insurance through taxes or through premiums. That antitax fervor, in other words, rules out in advance some practical approaches to the problem of covering the entire population at a lower cost.

This isn't the place to advocate any particular course of action. It could be that many readers of this book would content themselves with incremental adjustments to the current system of financing health care. Other readers might want to replace the whole system, root and branch, with government-sponsored, single-payer national health insurance. Still others might want to introduce a system of medical savings accounts. For the purposes of this book, I can remain agnostic on those disputes. My only point is that our American ideology, in addition to guiding us in certain directions, imposes blinders on us as well. We aren't as open to the full range of alternative possibilities as we might be, because our ideology rules out some of those possibilities that have been successful in other countries, or at least makes those possibilities suspect.

This excursion into health care is not an isolated case. I could take similar detours into many other public policy arenas. My main point, regardless of the location of the excursion, is that we Americans can learn from the experience of other countries. This doesn't mean adopting their approaches uncritically or being reflexively envious of other countries. We might conclude on examination, for instance, that the lust-to-dust welfare systems of most European countries impose a harmful burden on their economies and that our economy is vibrant, growing, and robust in part because we don't bear that burden. On the other hand, we might conclude that in some respects, American government capacity should be strengthened, not reduced (see Morone 1990:332–3). My plea, in other words, isn't simply to copy others but to study their practices and policies with a more open mind to see what we can learn.

PRAGMATISM

I have concentrated in this book on American traditions in political ideology and institutions. In a way, however, I'm arguing in this last chapter for a return to another venerable American tradition: pragmatism. Tocqueville even called a practical bent "the philosophical method of the Americans."

To be clear, ideas are important. Our individual political behaviors are not just driven by self-interest. And our collective public policy outcomes are not just the result of campaign contributions, the pursuit of votes, or interest group pressures. Instead, argumentation and persuasion also figure prominently into individual behaviors and policy outcomes. Ideologies, ideas, and values matter. There is a fairly substantial body of writing by now that argues for the importance of ideas in explaining political behaviors and public policy outcomes. (For reviews of this literature and reflections on the issues posed, see Kingdon 1993; Mansbridge 1990, 1993.)

Some of this writing on ideas makes the implicit assumption that reliance on ideas is a hopeful sign. We do better, the argument goes, if we rely on persuasion and rational deliberation than if we are driven by the pursuit of self-interest or pushed and pulled around by "political" considerations. I don't really share that assumption (Kingdon 1993). It seems to me that a lot of damage has been done over the course of human history in the name of some "good" idea. It appears that I'm not alone. Bellah et al. (1986:277) say that unease about "ideological fanaticism" is quite widespread. At any rate, I firmly believe that ideas are important. I'm less sure that this importance always turns out to be good.

So I want to argue here that we could profit from a return to pragmatism. Thoughtful observers often say that Americans, in addition to being principled, and in addition to being driven by certain distinctive values and orientations, have also been regarded traditionally as a practical, pragmatic people. Free and Cantril (1967:178), for instance, point to a "distinctive American pragmatism, pervading, shaping, and interpreting the American credo." We prize "know-how"; our biggest praise for a given approach is that it "will get the job done." In this pragmatic vein, we don't fully trust rigid ideologues; we regard them as a little bit suspect or "extreme."

As we should. Let me discuss two examples of ideology getting in the way of doing something sensible. The first is our Corporate Average Fuel Economy (CAFE) regulations (see Nivola and Crandall 1995). Suppose that we want, as a nation, to discourage the profligate consumption of fossil fuels, both to conserve energy and to reduce pollution. We know that a big proportion of such consumption is in the transportation sector. Americans commute long distances to work, for instance, each single individual driving a gas-guzzling automobile (or, lately, sport utility vehicle).

A perfectly straightforward way to discourage gasoline consumption is to do what every other industrialized country does: raise the price of gas. Those countries accomplish that goal by imposing taxes on gasoline that are extremely high by American standards, with the result that gas at the pump often costs two, three, and even four times as much as it costs in the United States. In the process, gas taxes generate government revenue that can be used for pressing national needs like transportation infrastructure, public transit, education, health care, and the like.

But the prevailing American ideology I have described in this book gets in the way of so sensible an approach. Remember that we regard taxes as confiscating what's ours. In addition, we prize our individual autonomy, and think of the privilege of driving our cars around the countryside as much, as often, and in whatever manner we see fit almost as a right. A dramatic boost in the price of gas, this thinking would conclude, would be an infringement on this individual autonomy, to which we believe we are entitled. Thus the American suspicion of government, our unusual aversion to taxation, and our individualism all militate against the straightforward, simple, and efficient approach of raising the price of gas.

If you have any doubt about the way this works, consider the instance of the temporary spike upward in the price of gasoline in the spring of 1996. Politicians fell all over themselves to posture about bringing down the price. President Clinton released crude oil from the nation's petroleum reserve and ordered Energy and Justice Department investigations. Senator Dole, the Republican nominee for president, pushed for a repeal of 4.3 cents of the gasoline tax. Never mind that these measures would do almost nothing to affect the price of gas at the pump. Never mind also that the spike upward was driven by such factors as the long winter, which diverted crude oil into home heating oil, and the substantial short-term reduction of California refining capacity; neither of these could be affected by federal government policy changes. Americans just don't tolerate high gas prices or taxes very well (see Krauthammer 1996).

So instead of the high gas taxes that every other country levies, the United States has tried to accomplish energy conservation by a less direct approach, with the CAFE standards. The CAFE program requires each automobile manufacturer to produce a fleet of cars each year that achieves a prescribed average fuel economy. They can't produce only gas guzzlers; each manufacturer must also include some more fuel-efficient cars in its mix of models. This approach has the political virtue of imposing costs much less visibly and directly than a high gas tax would. Individual drivers aren't reminded of the cost every time they fill up at the pump.

But the CAFE approach builds in a lot of perverse inefficiencies, as Nivola and Crandall (1995) demonstrate. Manufacturers may build a certain number of smaller cars, for instance, but there's no discouraging their owners from driving as far and as fast as they can, thus burning gas. Consumers get around the standards by such devices as buying trucks or truck-like vehicles that aren't part of the regime. There's always the option of souping up the car after it's manufactured. None of these evasive measures would work if gasoline prices were really high: The more you would consume, the more you would pay. Meanwhile, CAFE regulations have their own burdens—paperwork, testing of automobiles, demonstrating that the requirements are being met, and the like.

Again, American ideology militates against a straightforward, practical policy in favor of a convoluted, inefficient, and ultimately ineffective approach. We could do with less adherence to this ideology of limited government and low taxes, and with more pragmatism. Furthermore, to be practical about it, we could "get the job done" much more directly and efficiently, by raising gas taxes.

My second example of the excesses of ideology is the takeover of the House of Representatives by the Republicans in 1994, the first time in forty years that the Republicans controlled the House. Most of them had signed the principles contained in the Contract with America, a document promising that if elected, they would vote for and work for various changes in public policy, like a balanced budget constitutional amendment, lower taxes, campaign finance and lobbying reform, welfare reform, and many other measures. They didn't regard these principles as a bunch of empty campaign promises. So when Republicans captured majorities in both the House and the Senate, the House Republicans set about to enact the Contract's provisions.

One of their problems was President Clinton. After quite a lot of intense negotiation, the conservative ideologues among the House Republicans did reach compromises with the more moderate Senate Republicans on many issues. But President Clinton vetoed the Republican versions of a seven-year budget-balancing plan, welfare reform, tax cuts, and several other bills that they had passed. He also vetoed several of the annual appropriations bills, without which government agencies cannot operate. Republicans decided to challenge Clinton over those annual appropriations by refusing to pass bills that he was willing to sign. As a result, the federal government partially shut down for an unprecedented several weeks on two different occasions in 1995–96.

The Republicans hadn't counted on what happened next. The public blamed them, not the president, for the impasse and shutdowns. Republican members of Congress thought that the election of 1994 had given them a mandate to enact the provisions of the Contract with America, and they further believed that the public, tired of politicians who don't deliver on their promises, would approve of the lengths to which they went to stand by their principles. Quite the opposite happened. The public, as far as can be judged by opinion polls, was uneasy about the Republicans' ideological rigidity and would actually have preferred them to compromise on their principles and promises more than they did. Finally, the Republicans did pass appropriations bills that the president signed, and the federal government finished out the fiscal year without further disruption.

The 1996 negotiations between the Republicans and the administration on a balanced budget by the year 2002, on the other hand, fell apart amidst bitter recrimination. Democrats accused Republicans of cutting Medicare to finance tax cuts for the rich. Republicans accused President Clinton of generating balanced budget proposals by using deceptive accounting gimmicks that wouldn't work and charged Democrats with failure to make fundamental changes in Medicare and Medicaid. So in 1996, everybody put off multiyear budget-balancing plans.

Part of this story, of course, was a matter of electoral calculation. The Democrats figured they could paint the Republicans as extremist enemies of Medicare. The Republicans figured that if they negotiated a balanced budget deal with President Clinton before the 1996 election, he would get the credit, not they. So it might be better to continue the impasse, complain to the voters that tax-and-spend Democrats were responsible, and claim that the only recourse would be to elect a Republican president in 1996 to go along with a Republican Congress.

But the other part of the story was the House Republicans' ideological rigidity. Many of them were convinced that they were right and that the electorate had sent them to Washington to stick to their principles. So they took the position that they were not going to compromise, even if it meant shutting down the government, taking a bath in the polls, casting their own reelection chances into considerable doubt, and placing their presidential nominee in a difficult spot. The result was that they not only paid an electoral price but also failed to achieve much of what they had set out to accomplish. A little pragmatism and flexibility would have gone a long way, in both electoral and public policy terms.

Many of the House Republicans realized the disadvantages of ideology and the virtues of pragmatism just in time. At the end of the session in 1996, the Republican Congress passed a flurry of legislation, including welfare reform, an increase in the minimum wage, the Kassebaum-Kennedy health care bill, telecommunications reform, and appropriations bills—all of which President Clinton signed. Incumbents could then go back to their constituents and fend off charges that they had accomplished nothing. Republicans did lose seats in the election of 1996, but they managed to retain control of the House. And impressed with the virtues of pragmatism, they negotiated and passed a balanced budget and tax package in 1997. Pragmatism and compromise served them much better than ideology and "standing on principle."

Both of these stories—the CAFE standards and the actions of House Republicans in 1995–96—illustrate the virtues of pragmatism and the burdens of ideological rigidity. Emphasizing those virtues runs directly counter to many people's gut reactions. They prize "standing up for what you believe in," and "profiles in courage." My point is not that people shouldn't stand by their principles, or that they shouldn't believe firmly in their values. Of course policy decisions must be guided by principles. And of course vigorous debates about fundamental values are central to democratic processes. It's just that people should come to the point at which they ask themselves whether they're achieving their goals in a sensible way (see Gilmour 1995).

Contrast these two stories of ideology getting in the way of action with a pragmatic approach to environmental policy that learns from experience and eschews ideological rigidity. Rabe (1997) points out that each of three general propositions—that federal environmental regulation is misguided, that regulatory authority should be devolved to the states, and that other countries' emphasis on consensus is superior—has some merit. But in crucial respects, each is wrong as well. The Environmental Protection Agency (EPA) has actually launched several initiatives that deliver both environmental improvement and administrative flexibility; devolution has sometimes worked and has sometimes backfired, partly due to uneven state capacity and commitment; and some other countries' emphasis on consensus has actually not worked well in practice. An ideological stance that automatically decries the American environmental regulatory regime across the board misses such subtleties. What is needed instead is a hard-headed, practical examination of the conditions under which regulation, devolution, and consensus work and the conditions under which they do not. Rabe (1997:233) concludes that "the greatest challenge facing environmental policy analysts is avoiding the tendency for sweeping generalization and instead seeking a more systematic understanding of what does—and does not—work." A good dose of pragmatism would go a long way.

Huntington (1981) goes on to argue that American politics is characterized by periods of "creedal passion," including the original Revolution, the Jacksonian period, the Progressive period, and the 1960s. He says (1981:11), "America has been spared class conflicts in order to have moral convulsions." Hofstadter (1963:15) puts it this way: "The most prominent and pervasive failing [of American political culture] is a certain proneness to fits of moral crusading that would be fatal if they were not sooner or later tempered with a measure of apathy and common sense." Huntington (1981:39) believes that this situation is directly attributable to the American Creed, because any governmental or political regime must include some elements of hierarchy, power, and superordination and subordination, the very things that the American Creed challenges. In some respects, therefore, Huntington finds that the American Creed may be unworkable, and that there is an inherent gap between American ideals and American practices.

It is beyond the scope of this brief book to sort out fully the ways in which the prevailing American ideology serves us well or ill. On the up side, the American economy surely looks robust these days (as of early 1998), featuring steady economic growth, low inflation, and low unemployment compared to most other industrialized countries. Part of this performance can reasonably be attributed to American ideas about how a capitalist system should work. American business firms can lay off employees and trim payrolls largely at will, for instance—latitude that not all countries share. The same latitude equally implies a certain American ruthlessness and job insecurity, which probably does some damage to our social fabric. But it also does result in an ability to adapt to changing markets and a potential for greater leanness and efficiency.

But there are down sides as well. That same economy, for instance, produces a far greater gap between rich and poor than is found in other countries. The American tendency to regulate and rely on courts, rather than to tax and spend and rely on bureaucrats, produces the inefficiencies, inequalities, and even perverse results that we have discussed. The less ambitious public policy regime results in significant gaps in attention to such basic needs as health care, housing, and transportation.

American distrust of government also has the ironic consequence of weakening government capacity to the point that a self-confirming cycle sets in. Americans don't trust government, so they don't invest in it, so government doesn't work as well as it might, and the fears that government can never get anything right are thereby confirmed (see Morone 1990:332).

This cycle may even help explain low voting turnout in the United States, since a relatively weak and ineffective government promotes the view that participation won't matter anyway. Reforms aimed at weakening political parties, furthermore, combined with the advent of mass media technologies that allow politicians to appeal directly to voters without party intermediaries, have also diminished turnout (Rosenstone and Hansen 1993). To the extent that people used to vote because the party organizations brought them to the polls, decline in those organizations has contributed to the decline in turnout. Again, distrust of government and politics has its disadvantages.

Here's a very rough first cut at figuring out the pluses and minuses of the prevailing American ideology: American ideas work well in economic spheres—resulting in capitalist efficiencies, economic growth, high employment, job creation, low inflation, and generally admirable performance and competitiveness—but less well in spheres of social policy, where they result in inequalities, inattention to disadvantaged people, persistent poverty in the richest country on earth, and unnecessarily complicated regulatory and tax regimes. As I noted above, for example, instead of directly subsidizing social purposes, American public policy tends to regulate the private sector or to use tax credits and deductions, thereby introducing unnecessary ineffiencies and distortions.

But I'm not entirely confident even of that rough and ready distinction between economic and social spheres. Indeed, my difficulty in assessing the pluses and minuses of the prevailing American ideology may illustrate a more important point: Perhaps there is no way to make such an evaluation in the abstract. A struggle to state a set of general principles that would govern decisions about when the state is too big or too small, when government interventions in the economy and society are or are not appropriate, how balances between freedom and equality should be struck, and so on may be futile. Neither an impulse to devise government solutions to social and economic problems nor a stance that maintains that government never gets anything right serves us well. It's possible, in any event, that we should be guided by pragmatism and experience rather than ideology, abstraction, or general principles.

There is an additional reason for greater pragmatism: our institutions. Our fragmented system, with separation of powers, checks and balances, bicameralism, federalism, and weak political parties, is extremely hard to mobilize and lead. We could dream of a parliamentary system, and some Americans have. How different things are in Britain, for instance. Tony Blair's New Labour won an election one day, was installed in office the following morning, and within days thereafter took such dramatic steps as turning control of setting interest rates over to the central bank: Bang, bang, bang, just like that.

But parliamentary systems have their disadvantages as well, including less flexibility and a tendency to sharp changes in public policies following election results. Even if we wanted a parliamentary system, furthermore, the possibility of actually fashioning one in the United States is extremely remote. We could make our institutions a bit more conducive to mobilization at the margins if we wanted to. The U.S. Senate, for instance, could act to trim the considerable ability of individual senators to tie the institution up in knots if it were to adopt a rules change to end filibusters more easily and abandon the practice of allowing individual senators to put holds on nominations and bills. Even those marginal measures, however, would take a considerable investment of political credit and energy.

If we won't see a fundamental change in the structure of our institutions, and I'm confident that we won't, then pragmatism and "common sense" are the only ways to run them. As the House Republicans discovered, insisting on ideology to the point of sinking along with the ship neither accomplishes one's objectives nor serves one's electoral interests. Negotiating the bargains and cutting the deals necessary to run government in this terribly fragmented institutional setting takes a good bit of ideological flexibility and a considerable willingess to compromise on one's principles.

But pragmatism, in my view, does not necessarily imply either incrementalism, or compromise, or any particular ideological stance. Upon a hardheaded, practical examination of a given policy, we might well conclude that radical change is needed and that small, incremental steps won't do. Some such changes might move in a direction that convention would describe as "conservative," others as "liberal." A searching examination might lead us to scrap the tax code and replace it with a radically simpler system, for instance, whereas a similar consideration might lead us to comprehensive national health insurance. In other cases, incremental adjustments might work. I don't think a pragmatic approach, in any event, necessarily leads to incrementalism, to automatic compromise, or to any particular ideological position. And history shows us that huge, nonincremental policy changes are possible even in this system.

Again, I think that too great an insistence on the "American way" prevents us from learning from the experience of other countries. But more than that, it prevents us from being straightforward and sensible. We substitute convoluted regulation for direct government programs, for instance, or an impossibly complex tax code of deductions and credits for straightforward government subsidies. Ideology in general has its down side. The prevailing American ideology in particular also has specific disadvantages. A little pragmatism can go a long way.

THE FUTURE

In some respects, the prevailing American ideology I have described in the pages of this book has served us beautifully. There's a good bit of writing (e.g., Nivola 1997) to the effect that the American economy is particularly robust, with excellent growth rates and rather low unemployment by international standards. Part of the reason for this relative economic health might be that less of the American economy is tied up in the public sector, including various aspects of a welfare state such as pensions, health care, and family allowances. Suspicion of government has also led to less government regulation, at least in such areas as employment practices and retail trade. As the American economy has performed well compared to other economies in the last decade or so, other countries have been trying to emulate the United States in some respects—seriously considering downsizing government, paring back their social welfare commitments, privatizing functions that have been governmental, and lessening the burden of regulation.

As the economists say, however, there's no free lunch. We Americans pay a price for our ideology and our practices. We don't cover our entire population with health insurance. We tolerate a much greater gap between rich and poor, and have persistent poverty despite being the richest country on earth. We have less impressive commuter and long-distance passenger rail services. Other countries provide for much longer paid vacations than we do and pay a price in economic inefficiency; but their citizens do enjoy their vacations. There are trade-offs to everything. Either explicitly or implicitly, other industrialized countries have chosen to provide various government benefits and to pay the price for them in higher taxes and some economic inefficiency. Americans have chosen to strike the balance in the other direction.

Regardless of how we assess the pluses and minuses of the American way of doing governmental business, we may well be entering a period in which we will become impressed with the problems which the prevailing American ideology does not help us address. The United States, like many other countries, is facing a set of new problems that may overwhelm our customary ways of thinking about the proper role of government and may prompt us to think about new directions. Conversely, in an era of increasing global interdependence, other countries may find that they must change their customary ways of doing business. As trade becomes more free, for instance, they may find that lengthy paid vacations hurt their competitiveness. Interdependence may prompt less national distinctiveness over the long run than has existed in the past.

The world is facing some stark demographic trends, for one thing. Population is growing exponentially. The World Bank projects that by 2050, there will be 9.8 billion people on earth, an increase of 73 percent from the current 5.7 billion and a quadrupling of the world's population in just one hundred years (*Washington Post* 1996). Increasing food production has allowed humankind to stave off mass starvation so far, although regional shortages of land and food have already produced starvation, refugees, and violent conflict in some instances (Brown 1997:115). Successfully dealing with this population pressure may require many countries to use a greater level of coordination and planning than has been used traditionally, and may require fundamental cultural, economic, and political changes.

Demographic trends affect industrialized societies in other ways. The population in the United States and in other industrialized countries is aging, for one thing. It used to be that there were plenty of American workers for every retiree on social security and Medicare, enough to finance these programs for older Americans through payroll taxes without undue strain. But by 1995, there were only three workers for every retiree, and by 2035 the ratio will shrink to 2:1 (Aaron 1997:19). Clearly, some adjustments are necessary. And the day of reckoning is fast approaching.

Every industrialized country is grappling with the same aging of the population. In fact, the United States is not in as serious a position as some others. By 2030, the ratio of people past age sixty-four to those aged fifteen to sixty-four will be about 30 percent in the United States, 40 percent in France and Great Britain, and 50 percent in Germany and Japan (Bosworth and Burtless 1997). Within the United States, furthermore, there will be fewer children and nonworking adults over time compared to the number of workers, which presumably frees resources to support retirees (Aaron 1997). So it's possible that the American crunch created by the retirement of baby boomers in the first half of the twenty-first century will be manageable if we plan for it, and will not require radical surgery. In this case, pragmatism may prompt incremental changes in social security, rather than entirely new approaches.

Another fact many people in industrialized countries do not fully appreciate is the extent to which they consume. Population growth itself isn't the only source of concern about the capacity of the globe's resources to support humankind. Consumption is also a problem. We're burning up scarce resources at a terrific clip, and most of that consumption is in industrialized countries. The annual population increase in the United States of 2.6 million people, for instance, puts more pressure on the world's resources than India's annual increase of 17 million, because Americans consume so much more food, steel, wood, and energy (Brown 1997:19). We may be approaching a time, though exactly when is far from clear, when we can't continue this sort of binge, because the globe won't sustain it.

If we are to address such a problem, the traditional American emphasis on individual autonomy, and the customary American suspicion of collective action and governmental initiative, may have to bend significantly. It's hard to imagine a way that both allows people to go their own way and still addresses this sort of societal and global problem.

But demographic trends and consumption aren't the only conditions that the traditional prevailing American ideology doesn't address very well. The country, indeed the entire world, faces a set of environmental problems that call for a more collective solution than our usual individual autonomy allows. It's pretty well understood by now that ozone depletion and greenhouse gases, for instance, are at least partly caused by the by-products of modern civilization. As we release chlorofluorocarbons (CFCs) into the upper atmosphere, we break down the ozone that protects us all. And as we burn fossil fuels, we create a greenhouse effect which contributes to global climate change. Global carbon emissions from the burning of fossil fuels have roughly tripled since 1960 (Brown 1997:10). Both trends—ozone depletion and global warming—at the most pessimistic estimates, could constitute disasters. Even at the most optimistic, they are serious problems.

Such problems as environmental degradation cannot be solved by letting everybody go their own way. Things like a clean environment or the national defense are, in the scholarly parlance, "collective goods," meaning that each person shares in the enjoyment of the good whether or not he or she contributes to its generation (see Olson 1965). I will enjoy cleaner air, for instance, whether or not I individually and voluntarily put a catalytic converter on my own car. I will be protected by the national defense system whether or not I volunteer to serve in the armed forces or voluntarily write checks to the Pentagon. In other words, when it comes to collective goods, I have every incentive to be a "free rider." I can save the price of the catalytic converter out of my own pocket, for example, secure in the knowledge that my individual converter won't increase my ability to enjoy clean air.

Individual autonomy will not provide for collective goods like environmental preservation or national defense. Societies, often through their governments, must either provide incentives for people to contribute or take measures to require them to do so. Incentives include effluent fees if a company discharges more than a certain amount of waste into a river, for example, or tax credits for installing insulation or solar heating. In the case of national defense, incentives include the GI bill and reenlistment bonuses to make military service more attractive. Requirements include mandating catalytic converters on new automobiles, instituting a military draft, or levying taxes to finance national defense. Both incentive and requirement strategies interfere with the individual autonomy Americans have traditionally prized.

As we become more aware of the global environmental costs of industrialized civilization, we may discover that we cannot afford the luxury of as much individual autonomy as we have been enjoying. "We" also refers to countries as well as individuals. The Europeans at the Earth Summit in June 1997, for instance, expressed their impatience with American hesitation over reducing releases of carbon dioxide, pointing out that climate change is a worldwide problem that defies national boundaries. And it is true that the United States, with 5 percent of the world's population, produces 23 percent of the world's carbon emissions, far more than any other country (Brown 1997:8).

The point is that we—countries and individuals—will be obliged to rein in our tendency to do our own thing, in the interests of preserving the environment for everybody and for future generations. We have already started this process through current environmental regulations and international agreements. Emissions of CFCs are falling, for instance, due to international efforts to protect the world's ozone layer (Brown 1997:151). Some agreements on greenhouse gases were reached in Kyoto, Japan, in 1997. We will have to continue with, and accelerate, these and other such efforts.

These environmental issues are but one manifestation of the larger process of globalization. The march of communications and transportation technology, for one thing, has shrunk the world. Countries have also become more interdependent economically. As I indicated toward the end of Chapter 4, a certain degree of isolation has historically enabled Americans to develop and nurture a distinctive tradition of individual autonomy and limited government. As countries become more interdependent, they must adjust to the practices of others.

In some respects, other countries may emulate the United States. The robust American economy looks in early 1998 to be the envy of the world. Other countries may find America's relatively limited government, small public sector, and laissez-faire free market system attractive. But in other ways, we may find it useful to emulate them. Given that our public sector is smaller than theirs, we do have some room to raise taxes for public purposes if that is what we choose to do. We may choose not to, for good political and economic reasons; I'm only saying that we could raise taxes if we wanted to. The degree to which we move in their direction, the degree to which they move in ours, or indeed the degree to which any movement takes place at all are all difficult to predict.

In the short run at least, however, there is increasing divergence rather than convergence, among industrialized countries, at least as measured by the differences among their public expenditures as a percentage of GDP (Rose 1991:213). Many European countries, furthermore, will resist efforts to trim the welfare state too far. In the 1997 French elections, for example, public unhappiness with the government's efforts to cut back on social programs to meet European monetary union requirements resulted in a solid victory for leftist parties. Similar unhappiness resulted in protests and moves to preserve the welfare state in several other European countries.

Increasing interdependence may conceivably produce more similarity across countries in the long run. If so, American distinctiveness will diminish. But the durability of both political culture and institutions will also preserve many differences among countries. It is hard to believe that most European countries, even in the face of admiration of the performance of the American economy, will abandon their welfare states and move to adopt a thoroughgoing American-style capitalist system. They will probably find ways to trim back their government programs rather than dismantle them. It's equally unlikely, actually more unlikely, that Americans will move in the direction of a lust-to-dust welfare state. In fact, the current direction in American politics is exactly the opposite.

As we continue the process of increasing global interdependence, we may find that we will not necessarily be forced to make a stark choice between American-style relatively unfettered capitalism with limited government and European-style social programs and economic interventions. It might be possible to have both robust, growing economies and social programs and economic security (Pearlstein and Blustein 1997). But devising such an approach requires a bit of ideological flexibility. Just as the French may need to revise their policies of government intervention in such workplace issues as layoffs and hours, Americans may need to revise their views on government provision of various social benefits. But a happy medium may be possible if we are willing to consider pragmatically, in the light of experience, what works and what does not.

One major argument of this book has been that a set of historical circumstances produced the prevailing American ideology responsible for the manifestations of limited government in our public policies and institutions. If a theory of path dependence is right, then America will continue that tradition for a good long while. But a pattern of path dependence is also replete with new choices and possible new directions. If these historical circumstances change, as a result of either increasing globalization, for example, or overwhelming pressures of demographic or environmental problems, America will be forced to adapt. My hope is that there is enough pragmatism and flexibility left in the American political culture to enable us to adapt to changing conditions successfully.

References

Aaron, Henry J, 1997. "A Bad Idea Whose Time Will Never Come," *The Brookings Review*, Summer, pp 17–23.

Almond, Gabriel A., and Sidney Verba, 1963. *The Civic Culture: Political Attitudes and Democracy in Five Nations* (Princeton University Press).

Arthur, W. Brian, 1988. "Self-Reinforcing Mechanisms in Economics," in Philip W. Anderson, Kenneth J. Arrow, and David Pines, editors, *The Economy as an Evolving Complex System* (Addison-Wesley), pp 9–31.

Arthur, W. Brian, 1994. *Increasing Returns and Path Dependence in the Economy* (University of Michigan Press).

Bailyn, Bernard, 1967. *The Ideological Origins of the American Revolution* (Harvard University Press).

Balogh, Brian, 1991. "Reorganizing the Organizational Synthesis: Federal-Progressive Relations in Modern America," *Studies in American Political Devleopment*, 5:119–172.

Bellah, Robert N., Richard Madsen, William M. Sullivan, Ann Swidler, and Steven M. Tipton, 1985. *Habits of the Heart: Individualism and Commitment in American Life* (University of California Press; paperback edition, Harper & Row, 1986).

Borjas, George J., 1990. *Friends or Strangers: The Impact of Immigrants on the U.S. Economy* (Basic Books).

Bosworth, Barry, and Gary Burtless, 1997. "Budget Crunch: Population Aging in Rich Countries," *The Brookings Review*, Summer, pp 10–15.

Bridges, Amy, 1986. "Becoming American: The Working Classes in the United States before the Civil War," in Ira Katznelson and Aristide R. Zolberg, editors, *Working-Class Formation: Nineteenth-Century Patterns in Western Europe and the United States* (Princeton University Press), Chapter 5.

Brown, Lester R., et al., 1997. *State of the World* (W. W. Norton).

Burke, Thomas F., 1997. "On the Rights Track: The Americans with Disabilities Act," in Pietro S. Nivola, editor, *Comparative Disadvantages: Social Regulations and the Global Economy* (The Brookings Institution), Chapter 6.

Burtless, Gary, 1994. "Public Spending on the Poor: Historical Trends and Economic Limits," in Sheldon H. Danziger, Gary D. Sandefur, and Daniel H. Weinberg, editors, *Confronting Poverty: Prescriptions for Change* (Harvard University Press), pp 51–84.

Burtless, Gary, 1996. "Worsening American Income Inequality: Is World Trade to Blame?," *The Brookings Review*, Spring, pp 27–32.

017119

Cameron, David, 1978. "The Expansion of the Public Economy: A Comparative Analysis," *American Political Science Review*, 72:1243–1261.

Casper, Jonathan D., 1976. "The Supreme Court and National Policy-Making," *American Political Science Review* 70:50–63.

Converse, Philip E., 1964. "The Nature of Belief Systems in Mass Publics," in David E. Apter, editor, *Ideology and Discontent* (Free Press) pp. 206–261.

Dahl, Robert A., 1956. *A Preface to Democratic Theory* (University of Chicago Press).

David, Paul, 1985. "Clio and the Economics of QWERTY," *American Economic Review*, 75:332–337.

Downs, Anthony, 1960. "Why the Government Budget Is Too Small in a Democracy," *World Politics*, 12:541–556.

Epstein, Leon D., 1964. *British Politics in the Suez Crisis* (University of Illinois Press).

Evans, Peter, Dietrich Rueschemeyer, and Theda Skocpol, editors, 1995. *Bringing the State Back In* (Cambridge University Press).

Foner, Eric, 1984. "Why Is There No Socialism in the United States?" *History Workshop Journal*, 17:57–80.

Frank, Robert H., and Philip J. Cook, 1995. *The Winner-Take-All Society* (The Free Press).

Free, Lloyd A., and Handley Cantril, 1967. *The Political Beliefs of Americans: A Study of Public Opinion* (Rutgers University Press).

Gilmour, John B., 1995. *Strategic Disagreement: Stalemate in American Politics* (University of Pittsburgh Press).

Greenstone, J. David, 1969. *Labor in American Politics* (Knopf).

Hall, Peter A., editor, 1989. *The Political Power of Economic Ideas: Keynesianism across Nations* (Princeton University Press).

Hamilton, Alexander, James Madison, and John Jay, 1788. *The Federalist* (Modern Library edition, Random House, 1937).

Hartz, Louis, 1955. *The Liberal Tradition in America* (Harcourt, Brace).

Hattam, Victoria C., 1992. "Institutions and Political Change: Working-Class Formation in England and the United States, 1820–1896," *Politics and Society* 20:133–166.

Haveman, Robert, and Barbara Wolfe, 1994. *Succeeding Generations: On the Effects of Investments in Children* (Russell Sage Foundation).

Heclo, Hugh, 1986. "The Political Foundations of Antipoverty Policy," in Sheldon H. Danziger and Daniel H. Weinberg, editors, *Fighting Poverty: What Works and What Doesn't* (Harvard University Press).

Heidenheimer, Arnold J., Hugh Heclo, and Carolyn Teich Adams, 1983. *Comparative Public Policy: The Politics of Social Choice in Europe and America* (St. Martin's Press, Second Edition).

Hirschman, Albert O., 1982. *Shifting Involvements: Private Interest and Public Action* (Princeton University Press).

Hofstadter, Richard, 1963. *The Age of Reform: From Bryan to F.D.R.* (Knopf; first edition 1955).

Hofstadter, Richard, 1969. *The Idea of a Party System* (University of California Press).

Hofstadter, Richard, 1989. *The American Political Tradition: And the Men Who Made It* (Vintage Books; first edition, Knopf, 1948).

Howard, Christopher, 1997. *The Hidden Welfare State* (Princeton University Press).

Huntington, Samuel P., 1981. *American Politics: The Promise of Disharmony* (Harvard University Press).

Inglehart, Ronald, 1997. *Modernization and Postmodernization* (Princeton University Press).

Jackson, John E., and David C. King, 1989. "Public Goods, Private Interests, and Representation," *American Political Science Review* 83:1143–1164.

Jillson, Calvin C., 1988. *Constitution Making: Conflict and Consensus in the Federal Convention of 1787* (Agathon Press).

Kagan, Robert A., 1991. "Adversarial Legalism and American Government," *Journal of Policy Analysis and Management* 10:369–406.

Kagan, Robert A. and Lee Axelrad, 1997. "Adversarial Legalism: An International Perspective," in Pietro S. Nivola, editor, *Comparative Disadvantages? Social Regulations and the Global Economy* (The Brookings Institution), Chapter 4.

Katznelson, Ira, and Aristide R. Zolberg, editors, 1986. *Working-Class Formation: Nineteenth-Century Patterns in Western Europe and the United States* (Princeton University Press).

Katznelson, Ira, 1986. "Working-Class Formation: Constructing Cases and Comparisons," in Katznelson and Aristide Zolberg, editors, *Working-Class Formation: Nineteenth-Century Patterns in Western Europe and the United States* (Princeton University Press), Chapter 1.

Kinder, Donald R., 1983. "Diversity and Complexity in American Public Opinion," in Ada Finifter, editor, *The State of the Discipline* (American Political Science Association) pp. 389–425.

King, Anthony, 1973. "Ideas, Institutions, and the Policies of Governments: A Comparative Analysis," *British Journal of Political Science*, 3:291–313, and 409–423.

Kingdon, John W., 1989. *Congressmen's Voting Decisions* (University of Michigan Press, third edition; first edition 1974).

Kingdon, John W., 1993. "Politicians, Self-Interest, and Ideas," in George E. Marcus and Russell L. Hanson, editors, *Reconsidering the Democratic Public* (Pennsylvania State University Press) pp 73–89.

Kingdon, John W., 1995. *Agendas, Alternatives, and Public Policies* (Harper-Collins, second edition; first edition 1984).

Krauthammer, Charles, 1996. "A Nation of Crybabies," *Washington Post*, May 3, 1996, p. A21.

Lipset, Seymour Martin, 1977. "Why No Socialism in the United States?,"
in Seweryn Bialer and Sophis Sluzar, editors, *Sources of Contemporary
Radicalism* (Westview).

Lipset, Seymour Martin, 1979. *The First New Nation: The United States in
Historical and Comparative Perspective* (W. W. Norton; first edition,
Basic Books, 1963).

Lipset, Seymour Martin, 1990. *Continental Divide: The Values and Institutions of the United States and Canada* (Routledge).

Lipset, Seymour Martin, 1991. "American Exceptionalism Reaffirmed," in
Byron E. Shafer, editor, *Is America Different? A New Look at American
Exceptionalism* (Oxford University Press).

Lipset, Seymour Martin, 1996. *American Exceptionalism: A Double-Edged
Sword* (W. W. Norton).

Lowery, David, and William Berry, 1983. "The Growth of Government in
the United States: An Empirical Assessment of Competing Explanations," *American Journal of Political Science*, 27:665–694.

Mansbridge, Jane, editor, 1990. *Beyond Self-Interest* (University of Chicago
Press).

Mansbridge, Jane, 1993. "Self-Interest and Political Transformation," in
George E. Marcus and Russell L. Hanson, editors, *Reconsidering the
Democratic Public* (Pennsylvania State University Press) pp 91–109.

McCloskey, Herbert, and John Zaller, 1984. *The American Ethos: Public
Attitudes toward Capitalism and Democracy* (Harvard University
Press).

Morone, James A., 1990. *The Democratic Wish: Popular Participation and
the Limits of American Government* (Basic Books).

Nivola, Pietro S., editor, 1997. *Comparative Disadvantages?: Social Regulations and the Global Economy* (The Brookings Institution).

Nivola, Pietro S. and Robert W. Crandall, 1995. *The Extra Mile: Rethinking
Energy Policy for Automotive Transportation* (The Brookings Institution).

North, Douglass C., 1990. *Institutions, Institutional Change, and Economic
Performance* (Cambridge University Press).

OECD, 1996. Organisation for Economic Co-Operation and Development, *OECD Economic Outlook*, December 1996, Annex Tables 28 and
29.

Orloff, Ann Shala, and Theda Skocpol, 1984. "Why Not Equal Protection?
Explaining the Politics of Public Social Spending in Britain,
1900–1911, and the United States, 1880s–1920," *American Sociological
Review* 49:726–750.

Olson, Mancur, 1965. *The Logic of Collective Action* (Harvard University
Press).

Page, Benjamin I. and Robert Y. Shapiro, 1992. *The Rational Public: Fifty
Years of Trends in Americans' Policy Preferences* (University of Chicago
Press).

Pearlstein, Steven, and Paul Blustein, 1997. "In the Best of Both Worlds, Consider a Third Option," *Washington Post*, June 23, 1997, p. A12.

Perlin, George, 1997. "The Constraints of Public Opinion: Diverging or Converging Paths?", in Keith Bantin, George Hoberg, and Richard Simeon, editors, *Degrees of Freedom: Canada and the United States in a Changing World* (McGill-Queen's University Press), Chapter 3.

Pierson, Paul, 1994. *Dismantling the Welfare State?: Reagan, Thatcher, and the Politics of Retrenchment* (Cambridge University Press).

Pierson, Paul, 1996. "Path Dependence and the Study of Politics," paper delivered at the annual meeting of the American Political Science Association.

Pocock, J. G. A., 1975. *The Machiavellian Moment: Florentine Political Thought and the Atlantic Republican Tradition* (Princeton University Press).

Putnam, Robert, 1995. "Bowling Alone: America's Declining Social Capital," *Journal of Democracy*, 6:65–78.

Quadagno, Jill, 1994. *The Color of Welfare: How Racism Undermined the War on Poverty* (Oxford University Press).

Rabe, Barry, 1997. "Comment by Barry Rabe," in Pietro S. Nivola, editor, *Comparative Disadvantages? Social Regulations and the Global Economy* (Brookings Institution Press), pp 232–237.

Rae, Douglas, et al., 1981. *Equalities* (Harvard University Press).

Ranney, Austin, 1965. *Pathways to Parliament* (University of Wisconsin Press).

Rohde, David W., 1991. *Parties and Leaders in the Post-Reform House* (University of Chicago Press).

Rose, Richard, 1991. "Is American Public Policy Exceptional?", in Byron E. Shafer, editor, *Is America Different? A New Look at American Exceptionalism* (Oxford University Press).

Rosenstone, Steven J. and John Mark Hansen, 1993. *Mobilization, Participation, and Democracy in America* (Macmillan).

Sandel, Michael J., 1996. *Democracy's Discontent: America in Search of a Public Philosophy* (Harvard University Press).

Schlesinger, Arthur M., Jr., 1986. *The Cycles of American History* (Little, Brown, third edition).

Shafer, Byron E., editor, 1991. *Is America Different? A New Look at American Exceptionalism* (Oxford University Press).

Shain, Barry Alan, 1994. *The Myth of American Individualism: The Protestant Origins of American Political Thought* (Princeton University Press).

Shefter, Martin, 1986. "Trade Unions and Political Machines: The Organization and Disorganization of the American Working Class in the Late Nineteenth Century," in Ira Katznelson and Aristide R. Zolberg, editors, *Working-Class Formation: Nineteenth-Century Patterns in Western Europe and the United States* (Princeton University Press), Chapter 6.

Shefter, Martin, 1994. *Political Parties and the State: The American Histori-cal Experience* (Princeton University Press).

Shklar, Judith N., 1991. *American Citizenship: The Quest for Inclusion* (Harvard University Press).

Skocpol, Theda, 1985. "Bringing the State Back In: Strategies of Analysis in Current Research," in Peter Evans, Dietrich Rueschemeyer, and Theda Skocpol, editors, *Bringing the State Back In* (Cambridge University Press).

Skocpol, Theda, 1992. *Protecting Soldiers and Mothers: The Political Origins of Social Policy in the United States* (Harvard University Press).

Skowronek, Stephen, 1982. *Building a New American State: The Expansion of National Administrative Capacities 1877–1920* (Cambridge University Press).

Smith, Rogers, M., 1993. "Beyond Tocqueville, Myrdal, and Hartz: The Multiple Traditions in America," *American Political Science Review,* 87:549–566.

Smith, Steven Rathgeb, 1995. "The Role of Institutions and Ideas in Health Care Policy," *Journal of Health Politics, Policy and Law* 20: 385–389.

Steinmo, Sven, 1993. *Taxation and Democracy: Swedish, British, and American Approaches to Financing the Modern State* (Yale University Press).

Steinmo, Sven, 1994. "American Exceptionalism Reconsidered: Culture or Institutions?," in Lawrence C. Dodd and Calvin Jillson, editors, *The Dynamics of American Politics: Approaches and Interpretations* (Westview Press).

Steinmo, Sven, Kathleen Thelen, and Frank Longstreth, editors, 1992. *Structuring Politics: Historical Institutionalism in Comparative Analysis* (Cambridge University Press).

Steinmo, Sven, and Jon Watts, 1995. "It's the Institutions, Stupid!: Why Comprehensive National Health Insurance Always Fails in America," *Journal of Health Politics, Policy and Law* 20:329–372.

Stimson, James A., 1991. *Public Opinion in America: Moods, Cycles, and Swings* (Westview Press).

Taylor, George Rogers, editor, 1972. *The Turner Thesis: Concerning the Role of the Frontier in American History* (D. C. Heath, third edition).

Temin, Peter, 1991. "Free Land and Federalism: American Economic Exceptionalism," in Byron E. Shafer, editor, *Is America Different? A New Look at American Exceptionalism* (Oxford University Press).

Thelen, Kathleen, and Sven Steinmo, 1992. "Historical Institutionalism in Comparative Politics," in Sven Steinmo, Kathleen Thelen, and Frank Longstreth, editors, *Structuring Politics: Historical Institutionalism in Comparative Analysis* (Cambridge University Press), Chapter 1.

Tocqueville, Alexis de, 1835. *Democracy in America* (edited by Richard Heffner, Penguin, 1956).

Topel, Robert H., 1997. "Factor Proportions and Relative Wages: The Supply-Side Determinants of Wage Inequality," *Journal of Economic Perspectives* 11:55–74.

Turner, Frederick Jackson, 1920. *The Frontier in American History* (Holt).

Verba, Sidney, and Gary R. Orren, 1985. *Equality in America: The View from the Top* (Harvard University Press).

Walker, Jack L., 1991. *Mobilizing Interest Groups in America* (University of Michigan Press).

Washington Post 1996. "What on Earth?," July 20, 1996, p. A21.

Weaver, R. Kent, 1985. *The Politics of Industrial Change* (The Brookings Institution).

Weaver, R. Kent, and Bert A. Rockman, editors, 1993. *Do Institutions Matter?: Government Capabilities in the United States and Abroad* (The Brookings Institution).

Weir, Margaret, 1992a. *Politics and Jobs: The Boundaries of Employment Policy in the United States* (Princeton University Press).

Weir, Margaret, 1992b. "Ideas and the Politics of Bounded Innovation," in Sven Steinmo, Kathleen Thelen, and Frank Longstreth, editors, *Structuring Politics: Historical Institutionalism in Comparative Analysis*, Chapter 7 (Cambridge University Press).

Weir, Margaret, Ann Shola Orloff, and Theda Skocpol, editors, 1988. *The Politics of Social Policy in the United States* (Princeton University Press).

White, Joseph, 1995a. *Competing Solutions: American Health Care Proposals and International Experience* (The Brookings Institution).

White, Joseph, 1995b. "The Horses and the Jumps: Comments on the Health Care Reform Steeplechase," *Journal of Health Politics, Policy and Law*, 20:373–383.

Wilson, Graham K., 1998. *Only in America: The Politics of the United States in Comparative Perspective* (Chatham House).

Wood, Gordon S., 1969. *The Creation of the American Republic: 1776–1787* (University of North Carolina Press).

Wood, Gordon S., 1992. *The Radicalism of the American Revolution* (Knopf).

Young, James P., 1996. *Reconsidering American Liberalism: The Troubled Odyssey of the Liberal Idea* (Westview Press).

Zuckert, Michael P., 1994. *Natural Rights and the New Republicanism* (Princeton University Press).

Zundel, Alan, 1995. "The Civic Republican Challenge to Liberalism: The Past, Present, and Future of American's Submerged Tradition," paper delivered at the annual meeting of the American Political Science Association.

Index